*You May Lose
Your Balance,
But You Can
Fall Into Grace*

You May Lose Your Balance, But You Can Fall Into Grace

Finding Spiritual Renewal

In Life's Quirky Moments

Angela Payne

New Hope Publishers

Birmingham, Alabama

New Hope Publishers
P. O. Box 12065
Birmingham, AL 35202-2065
www.newhopepubl.com

Library of Congress Cataloging-in-Publication Data

Payne, Angela
  You may lose your balance, but you can fall into grace : finding
spiritual renewal in life's quirky moments / by Angela Payne.
     p. cm.
  ISBN 1-56309-725-7 (softcover)
  1. Christian women—Religious life. 2. Spiritual life—Christianity.
I. Title.
  BV4527 .P387 2002
  248.8'43—dc21

Cover design by Cathy Lollar

ISBN: 1-56309-725-7

N024102• 0802 • 5M1

DEDICATION

Irene Grace Brown

You have helped me to stand when I have fallen.

My heart is warmed by your love and touched by

His grace that you have so freely shared.

You are a priceless gift to me and to our family,

always bringing color and laughter to our home.

With love, respect, and gratefulness,

I dedicate this book to my own very special mother.

Table of Contents

Introduction

My young niece once inquired of her mother why I always asked if my hips looked big after trying on an outfit. Any outfit. My sister laughed and told her it was almost like a family tradition. It had been happening as long as she could remember. This particular bodily measurement has been a consistent concern for me my entire life. Okay. It's really been an obsession.

The question that readily springs from my lips comes without hesitation or even awareness. It is like breathing. However, if the answer is affirmative, my somewhat stable emotional state is shattered. In fact, it plummets, until I begin the next step of my drama...the hasty changing of multiple outfits until a loose-fitting garment has adequately veiled the subject of my pain. If my hips are covered, my spirits will be somewhat improved. Although their circumference may not have changed, at least the width is somewhat camouflaged—less conspicuous perhaps. But the big problem has not necessarily gone away!

I am sometimes that way about other areas of my life. There are things I want to cover up—characteristics I would like to ignore and forget. But that unsanctified sin nature of mine has a way of squeezing out of its proper boundaries in the most unexpected and untimely ways. And although I might try to dress up these rather unpleasant characteristics with religious frills, they are still ugly. Plain old ugly. And ever so ready to perform if given even the slightest window of opportunity. My sin nature still has a way of hanging on as tightly as a pair of jeans that haven't been stretched out after a tumble in the dryer.

Ahhhh, but that is where His grace comes in. Actually, it has never gone away. It is just that sometimes I choose my way instead of His. And so do you. But what we all have in common is that when we lose our balance, we can fall into His grace. And that is when falling can be sweet.

If we are honest about how far we fall short in being what we are called to be, we really are a step closer to Truth. You know, the kind of Truth that lets you be free to admit that you have a propensity to love yourself more than you love Jesus or anyone else. And that sometimes, you are more religious than holy. Or more committed to studying God than enjoying Him. Think about it. Somehow we would rather dress up or camouflage our sins with religious rites, trying to hide them. Or I do anyway.

If you are altogether perfect and spiritually polished, you probably will not be able to relate to my stories. But if you are like me—quite flawed and very imperfect, but ever reaching up to accept the wild and exuberant grace of God—perhaps you will enjoy reading with me for a while. And I hope that you will be encouraged in remembering that although we may stumble and fall along the way, He loves us. Period. And no matter how hard or how many times we fall, He leans into our lives to help us get up. And with joy in His eyes and tenderness in His voice, He encourages us to continue along the path of the life He has set before us. He smiles before sending us on our way. And almost as an afterthought, He laughs and says, "Oh, and don't forget to enjoy the journey!"

Stumbling Into Grace Is Worth the Fall

Stories of experiencing God's blessings,
even on life's detours

Rug Fuzz

"As for me, I will call upon God,
and the Lord shall save me.
Evening and morning and at noon I will pray,
and **cry aloud**, *and He shall hear my voice.*
He has redeemed my soul
in peace from the battle that was against me."
Psalm 55:16–18a *(emphasis mine)*

The fuzz from my hooked rug filled my nostrils. Typically, I walk across this floral piece that adorns the floor at the end of my bed. But this was not an average day. I had just received news of an updated deadline on a writing contract. Instead of excitement and anticipation, I found myself having what can best be described as an emotional spasm. It is similar to a seizure. The symptoms range from fear, dread, tormenting panic, facial tics, to an overwhelming urge to throw up. This is a common reaction in the life of many writers, I have since learned. I appreciate knowing that many other creators of artistic and musical venues wrestle with the same monsters that I have encountered—the ones that eat you alive and then burp with satisfaction.

There was no place to run and hide, so I panicked like most people do when jolted by fear. There is one mandate in the Bible that I have never had trouble obeying: *"Cry Aloud."* It is one of my most treasured commandments, one to which I submit without hesitation or compromise. On this day, not only did I cry aloud; I *wailed.* But I did so into my rug at the bottom of my bed, fearing my neighbors would hear and curiously inquire about my psychological status. Besides, my hardwood floors hurt my nose. This was not a little panic I was having, but consuming fear leading to sure emotional disintegration.

"God have mercy, Christ have mercy," was all I could sob between ghastly and unintelligible utterances.

The terror of failure (and all of the other little demons that seem to come in a package deal with fear) was particularly highlighted to me that day. Making a career change while trying to support myself by writing and working as little as possible as a nurse has been a rather daunting transition for me. Often I have felt as if the timeless words from Psalm 56: 3–4 should be tattooed on my heart:

> *"When I am afraid, I will put my trust in Thee.*
> *In God, whose word I praise, in God I have put my trust;*
> *I shall not be afraid. What can mere man*
> *[i.e. editors, readers, audiences!] do to me?" (NASB)*

Fortunately, I managed to phone my sister, despite the mayhem going on at the foot of my bed. How she ever understood me is a miracle for which I am still thankful. She prayed until I could blow the rug fuzz out of my nose, and then reminded me that in my weakness His strength is made perfect (2 Cor. 12:9). I was a bonafide candidate. He had called me to the task and would certainly equip me to complete what was required.

I truly have learned to be grateful for moments such as I have described. They are a wonderful reminder of my weakness and His strength, and that I can do nothing apart from Him. Nor do I ever want to try.

Just recently, I read a description of a similar bout of terror in *The Mystery of Children* by Mike Mason, one of my favorite writers. He explained it as having recovered his primal scream: "All I remember is that I threw myself down on the floor, pounded my fists on the carpet and screamed. I recall exactly what I yelled. It was something like, 'Ahhhhhhhhhhhhh!!!!' followed by, 'God get me out of this!' over and over." He then says, "The first pounding was especially therapeutic. People yell at hockey games, but society needs more volunteers to lie prostrate on their own living room floors and beat the daylights out of their carpets."

I love Mike Mason. And I hope his wife does not mind. My admiration for him increased significantly because of his incredible transparency. I found it comforting indeed that I am not the only one who has a good wail on the floor. He goes on to share how that particular event was a signal time for change. He then got up from the floor and proceeded to make the adjustments the Lord was directing him to make.

Recognizing my weakness is my greatest step forward. There really is not one single thing I can do apart from Him other than fail, and that is exactly what Satan wants me to do. That was his strategic plan for me that day—to stay on the floor wailing and not get up. How would I deal with this fear that covered me like a black cloak, occluding my vision so that I groped in darkness and struggled to breathe?

Whenever our attention and energy become focused on our weaknesses, we are blinded from seeing His strength. Yes! We must be *aware* of our weakness, however, and very careful that we are not captured by those thoughts. If we don't quickly turn our focus to Jesus we will be overwhelmed. Paul wrote, "Be strong in the grace that is in Christ Jesus" (2 Tim. 2:1*b*). Our strength is in His grace. That is how we are to complete whatever task He has put before us.

If you have been paralyzed by fear and doubt, ask the Lord's forgiveness for losing your perspective and focus on His place of authority and Lordship. Fear separates us from Him. Our attention is shifted to ourselves or others. But even as King David cried out to the Lord during a time of fear, he begged, "Say to my soul, I am your salvation" (Psalm 35:3*b*). We should do likewise.

Charles Spurgeon elaborates in his book, *Morning and Evening*, explaining that David had doubts and fears, but he knew where to obtain full assurance—at the mercy seat. And I am quite sure he bowed before the Lord in his plea for mercy. That is one nice thing about being prostrate on the floor. You can't get much lower physically! Whatever the need, His grace is abundant, flowing freely from His mercy seat.

Ask. Receive.

And if needed, blow the rug fuzz from your nose.

PUSH

"My purpose will be established,
and I will accomplish
all my good pleasure."
Isaiah 46:10b, NASB

Saying good-bye to my patient and her husband, I thanked them for letting me be their nurse for the day. Not that they had anything to do in choosing me, it was just one of God's gracious blessings in their lives...or so I like to think. It had been a good day altogether. Although her labor had been slow, she continued to make progress. If things continued on course, she would deliver before I returned the next morning. Assuring them I would see their new little one before they were discharged, I said good night.

Much to my surprise, when I returned the following morning, my patient was still there. She had only just become complete in her dilation and was now ready to push. Not every woman is blessed to have wide hips like I do, and some have to really struggle to propel that bundle of joy through their more petite bone structures. This is a difficult feat, requiring the stamina and fortitude of something similar to a bulldozer in overdrive. Together, we worked persistently to thrust that baby into the world. The mom was like a machine, relentless in her effort to push her infant through the birth canal. During my examinations, I could feel his head even though I couldn't see it. Of *course* this was a male child! Why is it that we glean so many wonderful spiritual applications from the masculine gender? Especially as they get older! No woman would be the consecrated saint that she is today without the presence of men to enhance her spiritual journey.

This non-compliant and slow little guy provided a wonderful opportunity for me to learn something invaluable. I knew the Lord wanted to say something that was worth noting.

First of all, although we could not *see* him, we knew he was in there. Imagine me impatiently taking off my examination gloves while saying, "You can put your legs down, get dressed, and go home. Since we have worked this hard with no results, it is obvious we just *thought* you were pregnant. *If it is meant to be it will happen.*"

You are thinking, "Oh that is ridiculous. Absurd!" And rightfully so. Yet how often do we do that in our prayer life? We get tired and impatient, walking away without our "baby," so to speak. How easily we forget that "faith is the substance of things hoped for, the evidence of things not seen" (Heb. 11:1).

Someone once gave me a pin with this acronym:
Pray
Until
Something
Happens

This is such a wonderful parallel to our spiritual lives. We walk by faith and not by what we can see. We can't always comprehend what God is doing or understand His timing, but we continue to **PUSH**. Just as my patient did. Her husband held one leg back and I grasped the other one. There is not one thing graceful about a woman whose knees are wedged against her ears while she pants and puffs like a steam engine. But soon they were holding their precious and very cone-headed son!

First the *conception,* then the *waiting,* and then the *travail.*

And in her case, a lot of **PUSH**-ing. But the result was birth and new life! Some deliveries are more difficult than others, just like many of our prayers require more effort and tenacity than some. And in the process, we often get tired of praying and waiting and pushing. "Continue earnestly in prayer, being vigilant in it with *thanksgiving*" (Col. 4:2, emphasis mine). In other words: Having done all...**PUSH!** In the process, we can praise Him in advance for the outcome. We don't have to wait until we see it with our eyes to believe that His promises will be established and accomplished in our lives. Whatever God has conceived in your heart concerning His promises to you, hold fast and don't let go. Although it may be taking longer than you ever imagined, don't you even *think* about giving up!

PUSH!

Holy Discipline

"God disciplines us for our good,
that we may share in His holiness.
No discipline seems pleasant at the time,
but painful. Later on, however,
it produces a harvest of righteousness and peace
for those who have been trained by it."
Hebrews 12:10–11, NIV

The red sports car was trailing me, right on my bumper. The speed limit was 65, and I was tooling along between 55 and 60. Although the driver, with her bleach-blond spiked hair, looked annoyed, it did not bother me in the least that I was antagonizing her. After all, I was going the speed limit. By now I had accelerated up to 65 miles an hour. And she was still just a kiss away from my bumper. She glared at me. Stubbornly, I was more determined not to get into the other lane. My rationale was that I was going the speed limit and she didn't need to go any faster. At times I find my hypocrisy fascinating.

The Holy Spirit said to me, more loudly than the morning news I was listening to on the radio, "Angela, move over." And I ignored Him. "Angela, move over to the right lane so the girl can pass you."

"I must be hearing things. The Holy Spirit did not say that."

Continuing to race along with Ms. Blond Bomb hot in her pursuit to blow me off the road, I continued on my merry way at 65 miles an hour.

Again, "Angela, your pride is keeping you from giving in and moving over."

"You are right, Lord. But *she* shouldn't be going so fast."

On this particular lovely fall morning, I was returning from a wonderful Bible study led by my friend Barbara Barker. It starts at 6:15 AM, so obviously, it is very much worth attending to make the early effort. My childish reaction en route to my home that morning was no reflection upon her lesson about grace. I had even taken fabulous notes. And I was about to get a P.S. from God Himself that I would not quickly forget.

The day before, I had stopped in at an auto dealership to get my headlight changed. A simple fuse was all I needed. When I was quoted a price of $40.00, I laughed and walked away.

"Absurd. Ridiculous price. I'll change it myself." Admittedly, I had failed in my last attempt to change the headlight fuse, but suddenly I was challenged to try again. The manual made it look so very simple. Follow these easy steps—1, 2, 3.

That evening, after an hour of following the guidelines better than I have with most recipes, I considered writing to the wiseguy who wrote the manual and telling what I thought of his ridiculous instructions. Obviously he did not realize that he left out several steps on the headlight page. Slamming the hood in disgust, I made plans to give in and pay someone to change my headlight the next day. I did not realize that I had not closed my hood properly.

My P.S. from God happened during our ongoing conversation when He was prompting me to pull to the other lane of the highway. I continued to do my own thing. Suddenly, without warning, the hood of my car went flying up faster than an escaping helium balloon, rebounding against my windshield. It was not blue sky that I was looking at but rather a bright cobalt hood. That was all I could see until I peered down and looked between the two-inch crack above my motor. Slowing my speed down significantly, I saw Ms. Blond Bomb go flying around me.

"Now why didn't she do that earlier," I muttered.

You may think I reacted in an angry outburst. No, I was quiet and calm as I pulled over and secured my hood properly. I didn't feel condemnation, just a sort of peaceful chastisement.

My stubbornness cost me nine hundred and fifty-six dollars, although I did find someone to change my headlight fuse for ten dollars. At least I saved thirty dollars on that aspect. Technically, then, my whole ordeal only cost nine hundred and *twenty*-six dollars.

So when will I learn to obey quickly and promptly? I'm not sure. It is a shame that it takes me so long to catch on. And I really can't afford to be stubborn at the rate of almost a thousand dollars a lesson. The older I get the more I realize how much further I have to go. Maybe not in years, because those are passing faster than the Cahaba River outside my back door during the flood season. These little outbursts can happen so unexpectedly, just when I am really feeling so spiritual. For me, one of the most encouraging messages of God's grace is that it is always liberal and abundant, even when I am slow and obtuse. Sometimes it's just good to look back and see from where you have come.

He loves me, therefore He continues to discipline me. "My son [daughter], do not make light of the Lord's discipline, and do not lose heart when He rebukes you, because the Lord disciplines those He loves, and He punishes everyone He accepts as a son [daughter]" (Heb. 12:5–6 NIV). He doesn't give up on me. His grace is the gift that keeps on giving.

And whether it feels good to pay a thousand dollars or whatever consequence of disobedience comes my way, it is a reminder to pray, "Lord, give me a heart that obeys you quickly."

His discipline is His grace.

Internet

*"Guard the goo
that was entrust
guard it witl
of the Holy Spirit ?
2 Timothy ...*

While searching the internet for some travel services, ...
eyes were drawn to the image that was being presented.
Instead of airfares, a woman with a very seductive and provocative look on her face appeared on my computer. She had what
I call that classic "come hither" look. "What in the world," I
muttered. Suddenly, I realized that I had inadvertently pulled
up a pornographic site. How I went from a potential ski trip to
her remains a mystery. My first reaction was disbelief. My second was curiosity. In those brief moments, I rationalized that
it would be okay for me to see what all of the indignation was
about related to the open sites of pornography. Surely it could
not be so bad as people were saying. Besides, I needed to be
intellectually informed.

Fortunately, the Holy Spirit took over the carnal cells of my
mind.

"NOOOOO!!!"

Yelling aloud, as if there was an evil presence invading my
home (there was), I began punching keys furiously trying to
delete her pouty lips and bare chest. Her full mouth, partially
open, was smiling at me. Now I have seen a lot of nude women
in my career as a nurse, but never one like "Ms. Come Hither
Babe."

My home is a sacred place to me. It is a refuge from the

t our society calls "normal." Anger was spilling
realized how easy it was for me to access this site
en trying. The image continued to open up despite
nding the keyboard and shouting "NOOOO!" Putting
and on the screen to cover her, I finally managed to get
image turned off.

Staring silently at the blank screen for a few moments, I was amazed at both of my reactions to what had just taken place. It was the *curiosity* that astounded me more than the shrieking and frantic pounding of keys. There was a primal reaction to shield myself as if I were frightened. And I was frightened—of me. No, I am not attracted to women. That is not a problem. But her image represented a sensual and provocative nature that felt ominous and unclean.

Dirty.

Contaminated.

Not the sort of thing I wanted in my home or mind. As a single, I am forever being careful to keep my heart and mind pure sexually. But it would be *just* as important if I were married. The deluge of pornography in the last several years, in my opinion, has been an attempt of the evil one to pervert the physical union in marriage. Marital intimacy is the consummate expression of that which is holy in the heart and eyes of God. He is the one who created physical intimacy as a sacred act. *Of course* Satan wants to cheapen and pervert it. And our society continues to extend a warm and gracious invitation to him. Sadly, this attitude of permissiveness and openness has permeated countless Christian homes and hearts. Pornography has become an addiction for many women as well as men. Women might not be as drawn to visual images, but the reading of sensual books is a great weakness for many. Don't be lulled into thinking that nudity is the only classification of pornography. Sexual darkness creeps in slowly and insidiously, through the window of our eyes, in what we read, watch, and look upon.

While once walking home from a neighbor's house, it was so dark that I could not see the path. In just a couple of minutes of stumbling along, I noticed that my eyes were adjusting to the darkness. It's not because there was more light on the path, but because I had grown accustomed to my surroundings. It happened gradually.

This is the nature of sexual sin.

Slow

    Progressive

        Intensifying

Curiosity is part of our nature. But there is a costly price to be paid for some knowledge gained. "Oh be careful little eyes what you see..." This children's song carries more truth for us than it does them. For they have parents to turn off shows or take away books that fill their hearts and minds with impure thoughts. But for us, wizened adults who are sometimes too "grown up" for our own good, it is only our conscience and godly choices that will keep us free from sexual stains.

If your curiosity and acquired knowledge have hardened your heart toward the pure and lovely, ask Him for forgiveness and cleansing. Invite the Holy Spirit to daily make you sensitive to anything that is conflicting with purity and holiness. Desire that your heart and home be a sanctuary for His presence. Guard the deposit of purity that He entrusted to you with the help of the Holy Spirit. "Present your bodies a living sacrifice, holy, acceptable to God...And do not be conformed to this world, but be transformed by the renewing of your mind" (Rom. 12:1–2a).

Ask the Holy Spirit to show you these areas of darkness

where you have conformed, in subtle and blatant choices in mind and attitude toward sexuality. Paul gives a plea for purity to the church of the Thessalonians, encouraging them to possess their own bodies in purity and honor. It is all a work of His grace and our yielding. Turn away from that which will stain your heart and mind. Be eager to flee...to run...to hide from sexual darkness.

You will face blatant sensual intrusions such as my afternoon at the computer. But what about the steamy or suggestive television shows that are eagerly accepted, applauded, and embraced, not only by our society but also by Christians? What of the checkout line at the grocery store where the latest discovery for the ultimate sizzling sex life is in front of you? Do you turn away or read out of curiosity?

May each of our hearts long for purity of heart and mind. Just as we want to protect our children's innocence, may we be as careful to safeguard ourselves against the things that will so quickly defile our lives as adults.

Oh be careful *grown up* eyes what you see...for the Father up above is looking down in love, oh be careful *grown up* eyes what you see.

That #%$*@! Word

"And of His fullness we have all received,
and grace for grace."
John 1:16

My friend Dorothy told me of a recent prayer experience. All I could say was, "That is such a story of God's grace, such a sweet, sweet story of His grace." She had attended an evening of prayer at church. While praying alone, she felt impressed to go and pray for a woman she didn't know by name. In fact, she knew nothing about her life and had only seen her face at church. Introducing herself, she asked the woman if she could pray for her, and then knelt silently while listening to the Lord.

"Ma'am," Dorothy told the woman, "I know this may sound really strange, but the Lord wants you to know that it is okay for you to have a nice house. And He also wants you to know that He has heard the word *#@*!#@ before."

Even in recounting the story to me, Dorothy was incredulous. "Ange, I was as shocked that I said *that* word as she was when I said it! She looked at me in utter astonishment. Both of us were just staring at each other with our mouths open!"

The woman began to sob quietly and told Dorothy her story. She and her husband had just purchased a very nice home. Shortly thereafter, her twin brother had experienced grave financial difficulties. Consequently, he was in the process of selling his family's home and downsizing significantly. This woman was feeling guilty about her brother's situation, and thereby not enjoying or appreciating her new home. Because of the guilt, she couldn't see it as a gift to be enjoyed. The first part of what Dorothy shared brought comfort to her and peace from the onslaught of guilt.

The woman continued to speak. For years she had worked in an office where her peers knew she was a Christian. She had always been careful not to compromise her testimony. During a stressful event the week before, she had said a curse word, one of those really biggie ones, and had completely shocked everyone. Having the privilege of working with some good pious folks who hastily expressed more horror than grace and forgiveness, she had allowed the utterance of one word to become a mountain of failure and condemnation. And her Christian peers hadn't helped remove any of the rocks of judgement and condemnation that had added to the weight.

But Jesus came along through the voice of Dorothy, who was obedient to listen and follow His prompting.

And He said, "No, dear, I do not condemn you."

These are the same words He said to the woman caught in adultery, a woman the Pharisees were ready and willing to throw rocks at (John 8:3–11). "Let he who is without sin cast the first stone," Jesus told them. Jesus, full of compassion. Not the least bit taken aback that this woman had committed adultery, not once, but many times. He is the same unchanging Jesus, not the least bit shaken that his daughter had said a word that was something less than sanctified. Just as He unexpectedly comforted her in His love, He offers the same grace and comfort to you—whatever the struggle or failure might be.

That's just like Him—gracious in His grace.

A Trip to the Egg Bank

"But seek first the kingdom of God
and His righteousness,
and all these things
shall be added to you."
Matthew 6:33

From the time I reached my mid-twenties, I have encountered insensitive, bumbling, but nevertheless well-meaning and pleasant folks who offer their unsolicited thoughts about childbearing. "You know your biological time clock is ticking. You better hurry up and get busy."

Get busy.

Does that mean I make a quick trip to the fertility bank and make a deposit? "I would like to lay three eggs please."

Reminds me of days when my mother was on her organic kick and raising chickens for fresh eggs. The hens would make their morning offering and we would go out and gather them. It worked for them, but frankly, I would prefer a "rooster" to help me multiply the earth the old fashioned way. Or I suppose I could solicit donors. This can be done clinically and professionally, in the privacy of a cold and sterile medical clinic. Or my other option would be to follow the sage advice of the well-meaning and "get busy."

Now I have known some girls that "got busy." Completely frustrated waiting on God, they are now exhausted single mothers. No, I somehow don't think that even my age qualifies me to "get busy" with that which I have refrained from since my vow of abstinence at the onset of adolescence. Ahhh, the optimism of youth and innocence!

Actually, as far as this biological issue is concerned, I have handled it in the same way I have taken care of my snooze alarm every morning for most of my life. I simply punch it every time the obnoxious thing goes off. This daily routine has worked very well for me in the issue of the hormonal time clock as well.

At the age of thirty-five, I found that I needed to smack the snooze alarm of my ticking time piece with a little more regularity. But at the age of forty, my biological clock unexpectedly, cruelly, and viciously turned into a time bomb. Its alarming and relentless ticking threatened at any moment to explode, bringing destruction and finality to my dreams of family and children.

When we meddle, life gets muddled.

—Angela Payne

My journal sounds a bit morose during that period of time to say the least. My heart was wanting to trust and longing to hope, but I could not hear God's words. They were drowned out by the ominous and clanging time piece that I feared would detonate at any moment.

Finally I did hear His voice, louder than the clamor of alarms, but soothing, peaceful, comforting, loving. The Lord's compassionate words of tenderness were, "Be not afraid, trust in Me, let not your heart be troubled."

The One who gave me physical life and life eternal has not completed all of the chapters in my life. Yes, I could *get busy* doing things. Or I could *stay busy* fretting and fearing. And I have had those days. But I like these better. As I reaffirm the truth that my life is in His hands, that means my desire for motherhood as well. My Father, who knows the number of hairs on my head, is also counting how many eggs are in my ovaries! Perhaps a future journal entry will one day read...

*6:00 A.M. "I'm tired—exhausted. Lethargic. Incoherent. The children were awake all night throwing up. They did it in shifts. Right now they are stretched out on the bathroom floor sleeping. **Finally.** They are lying on the beach towels because I ran out of clean sheets. I'm afraid they got food poisoning from my left over stir-fry. I truly thought stir-fry lasted more than five days. My husband, for whom I waited so patiently for so many years, has been sleeping soundly for the last seven hours. He had **that look** in his eyes last night. Of course I said, "I thought you would **never** ask." Dr. Dobson warned me of days like this.*

That imaginative entry makes me smile in realization that when awaited desires are fulfilled, we are then introduced to another level of trust and opportunity for new and unexplored graces!

Every one of us is required to walk through vast areas of testing to reach spiritual maturity. Each will be unmatched and unrelated to another person's circumstances. We can't compare with one another. We find God's message of grace in whatever waves are pounding at us, threatening to capsize our life. We are all in the same boat!

In need of Him.

But our waves and storms will be different. And the climate of the water surrounding us may vary in degrees. These circumstances provide the opportunity to *trust.*

To hold tightly.

Joshua instructed the children of Israel before he died, "Hold fast to the Lord your God, as you have done to this day" (Josh. 23:8). He reminds them of all the things the Lord has done for them while encouraging, "Hold fast. Love the Lord. Be resolute and worship the Lord your God."

This issue has been an opportunity for me to run to God, and I do mean run. These days I am at a steady jog. Daily I must choose to trust in the Lord with all my heart, not being swayed by my understanding and interpretation of what is best for me. When we meddle and try to make things happen, or *get busy,* all we do is make a fine muddled mess. We can trust Him in all the details of our lives, especially His divine purposes. We seek Him first and not a plan, assured that He will add and complete all that He desires to our lives. And I really don't have to make a trip to the egg bank after all.

Song of Mercy

"I will sing of the mercies
of the Lord forever;
with my mouth will I make known
Your faithfulness to all generations."
Psalm 89:1

Catching sight of the policeman in the hedges, I slowed down and turned on my blinker, pulling into the nearest driveway. All of this happened before he had a chance to turn on his "blue light special." Zipping in behind me, we were soon exchanging the usual pleasantries one must have after offending the law. He was a handsome, pleasant officer and it was a beautiful fall day. It could have been sleeting and he could have been ugly. The combination of both might have been a most disagreeable state of affairs.

"Miss Payne, did you know you were going twenty miles over the speed limit?"

Readily I admitted that I did, enthusiastically adding that I was enjoying every moment of it. This is one of the rare times I was not speeding because I was late, but rather for the sheer joy of it. The day was gorgeous. Fall is the time of year that I come alive and fall in love with almost every man taller than I am. I was driving in a lovely area of town with curvy roads and beautiful trees. My windows were down and my hair was flying in my face. The air was fresh. It was one of those "inhale life" kind of days.

He looked at me as if to say, "You are just about the cutest thing I have ever seen." Or maybe that is what I thought since I was brushing hair out of my eyes.

Feeling quite conversational, I leaned out the window and said, "Do you hear the words to this song?"

He listened as I turned up the volume. Lynn DeShazo's soothing voice filled the speakers. It was no coincidence that she was singing "Mercy, Mercy Lord."

"That is what I would like to ask of you," I said, smiling. "Mercy. You see, I used to get several tickets a year for speeding. I even devoted part of a book I wrote in telling about it." I pointed to a copy that was in my front seat for validation. "But it has been *three* years since I have had a ticket." Giving him the most incredulous look, I repeated myself. "*Three years!* Can you *believe* that?"

He grinned and folded up his pad. Before walking away, he added, "Keep it in the speed limit."

Now I am not encouraging you to break the speed limit. On this particular day, I had violated the law and was guilty. And this was a moment of mercy. In the eyes of justice, I deserved a ticket. Truthfully, I could not deny that I was *enjoying* speeding. But doesn't Proverbs tell us that sin does bring pleasure for a fleeting moment, with the assurance of consequences? The appropriate one for me on this occasion would have been a hefty speeding fine. But I was granted mercy—which does not lessen my conviction to try to keep my speed within the limits.

The Lord has helped me slow my life down in so many ways in the last few chapters of my life. It has now been almost five years since I have received a speeding ticket. I do not claim that I have not gone over the speed limit since that day, for that would not be true. However, I have improved significantly. For much of my adult life, it was not uncommon for me to have at least two or three violations on my driving record. The process remains ongoing. But for the eternal record, God will continue to correct these areas and sometimes use tools such as men in blue suits. And He will for you, probably whether you ask for it or not. Yes, there will be consequences for our violations, but they will always be covered by His melodies of grace.

To you, oh Lord, I will sing praises.

The Grateful Rescue

*"Let us therefore come boldly
to the throne of grace,
that we may obtain mercy and find grace
to help in time of need."*
Hebrews 4:16

Checking my mail, I was happy to see an invitation to speak at a woman's retreat. It was to be held in a state that I especially enjoy visiting. My schedule allowed me to accept the request, and I marked the event on my calendar for the following year. About three months later, I received a rather large announcement with my picture on the front. Apparently it had been sent out to several hundred women within the association sponsoring the retreat.

I vaguely remember tossing it into a closet and continuing on with some immediate details of my life. Several months later, the coordinator for this particular state organization emailed me, asking for the title of my workshop. Upon reading her request I thought, "Oh, I must have misunderstood. I thought I was going to be the main speaker, but apparently I am just doing one of the workshops. *Ohhhhh.* Silly of me to have been confused." I considered contacting her for clarification, but decided against it, as I thought a question like that seemed a bit pretentious.

In the meantime, another women's group near the location of the retreat asked me if I would mind speaking to their group while I was in the area. I was happy to do so and sent an affirmative response, provided they could rearrange my flight. When I was picked up at the airport, I saw the same flier in the backseat that had been sent to me earlier—the one I had tossed into the closet and had not thought about since. "Now, why would they put just *my* picture on the circular without the rest of the workshop leaders? Interesting..."

After I finished my presentation to the group of ladies that Thursday night, I pulled aside a woman who I knew would be attending the fall retreat the following day. "Do you know who the main speaker is for the retreat this weekend?"

She questioned why I wanted to know.

I expressed my puzzlement about my picture, continuing to wonder why the other eleven workshop leaders were not shown.

Gingerly I asked, "Do you think *I* am the main speaker?"

She laughed, "Why surely you would know about it if you were!"

Well, of course. She was absolutely right. Nevertheless, I was anxious to see the schedule of the retreat. When we arrived there the next afternoon, I could feel my stomach tightening as I opened the welcome packet. And there it was:

Angela Payne—Friday Evening speaker 7:45

Angela Payne—Saturday Morning 9:30

Pulling my friend and confidant aside, I pointed to the brochure. She was silent and I was nauseated. The thought of feigning a fainting spell did cross my mind. "Anna, I will not be coming to dinner tonight, but I need you to pray for me." There was a small group of women that I had met the night before, and I asked her to please tell them as well.

And with that I went to my room and knelt before the Lord. Actually I was calm. Sort of. It was like that blanket of tranquility that I have heard people have before they are executed. I knew that unless He intervened, I could not get through the session that night or the one the next morning. And then there were the three additional workshops as well.

Now I am not an outline sort of girl, but I knew the Lord was directing me to make a framework of points. For the next hour I listened to Him and wrote. I revised it about three times and spent more time in prayer. Eating a handful of peanuts washed down with coffee, I was ready for the night's event. Actually, I was excited. I knew that I was at the mercy of God. And that was a good place to be. We know intellectually that we are always at His mercy, it's just that some occasions have a nice way of reminding us in our hearts.

The worship that night can only be described as an invitation into the very presence of the Lord. I experienced such a sweetness of holiness as three hundred women sang and worshiped together. And as I stood to share, I knew the Lord was with me. He was very near me.

These events are not what I would have chosen to happen. But that weekend stands out as one of those yellow marker-highlighted experiences, punctuated with exclamation points! He brought to mind Proverbs 19:21: "Many are the plans in a man's heart, but it is the Lord's purpose that prevails"(NIV). Following each session, I had the most wonderful and thrilling conversations with women whose hearts had been provoked by what I had shared. No, what *we* had shared. No, what *He* had shared through me.

As I left the next day, I had such a humble awareness of God's amazing grace poured into my life. He took any confidence that I might have had as a speaker and kindly reminded me that I could do nothing apart from Him. I would not claim that I was the most polished guest this organization has ever known. But I was, perhaps, the most grateful! I was so completely filled with the awareness of my need of God. It is really quite amazing that God can use any of us. Sometimes *with* our outlines and sometimes *despite* them! And we would be oh so wise never to forget it.

Whether it is in teaching young children, putting together a conference, speaking at one, or baking for it, we can do nothing, absolutely nothing, apart from His grace. At times, He may want to move beyond the constraints of schedules and plans.

Do we trust that God can take care of the details when an unexpected opportunity presents itself to us? He will. I have no doubt. Trust Him fully. We can bend with Him or get *bent out of shape*. Bending is much better.

I Like Your "Nos"

"'For My thoughts
are not your thoughts,
neither are your ways My ways,'
declares the Lord.
'As the heavens are higher than the earth,
so are My ways higher than your ways
and My thoughts than your thoughts.'"
Isaiah 55:8–9, NIV

Recently at a social dinner, I turned to one of my table mates and held out my wrist. "Check my pulse."

After a moment of assessing my heartbeat, she commented, "It's rather slow."

"I know! Isn't that wonderful?!" I said, joyfully.

Taken aback by my strange comment, she waited for me to continue. Leaning over, I explained, "One of the men that used to send me into cardiac arrhythmias is sitting in this very room! I am so grateful because not only is my heart not racing, but God loved me enough to say NO when I petitioned for this man in my life!"

So much has been given to me,
that I have no time to ponder over
that which has been denied.

—Helen Keller

I often reflect on a verse that is a good reminder during

times of disappointment or when I have not understood \
He has said no to my request:

"Now to Him who is able to keep you from stumbling,
And to present you faultless
Before the presence of His glory with exceeding joy,
To God our Savior,
Who alone is wise,
Be glory and majesty,
Dominion and power,
Both now and forever.
Amen. "
Jude 24, 25

He alone is wise. And because of His divine wisdom, He is able
to keep us from stumbling about with the decisions of our lives
even when they appear to be good. Although we don't understand why He has denied our request, we can be grateful. Why?
Because we trust His heart of love and wisdom. As we allow an
attitude of gratefulness to be enmeshed in our hearts as an
everyday expression of ourselves, we become joyful in heart.
Joy is not based on circumstances or feelings.

I love the famous quote by Winston Churchill that breathed
life and resolution into his people: "Never never never give
up." And I would add along with that premise, "Always always
always be grateful." This attitude requires great cultivation of
heart because the weeds of comparison, grumbling, and whining will always be there. I feel I am the "chief of all gardeners"
and must always be on the alert for sprouting weeds of
ungratefulness cropping up.

While praying for a friend one night in celebration of her
birthday, I said, "Thank you, Father, for the "*nos*" that you have

ssa." She asked me later, "What is so special about

the last several years that I have begun to appre-
ly times that the Lord has answered my requests
by saying "No, dear." At times I may whine and plead or pout,
but because of His love and wisdom, He continues to firmly say
no. He is the only wise God, the loving Father, the Good
Shepherd. And as much as I suspect I might just keel over and
die unless I get my way, He has promised that He withholds no
good thing from me. That which has my attention might look,
sound, and feel good, but His plan is even better. Trust Him.
Hold on to what He has promised—that He does not hold
back from you anything that is good for your life.

You can thank Him for your *nos*!

My Encounter
With Spider-Man

"Then He said to them, 'Follow Me,
and I will make you fishers of men.'
They immediately left their nets
and followed Him."
Matthew 4:19–20

M y sister once told me of having to drag my four-year-old niece out from under the bed for a spanking. Caroline had been slow and uncooperative in obeying her mother and was now about to be punished. Although she is a sweet child, especially when she is getting her way, she is not *always* docile. Just like the rest of us grown-up children. On this occasion, she was kicking and screaming with all of the energy and enthusiasm of a four-year-old. Her mother assured her that all of the flurry of activity would only enhance her moment of tribulation. This did not persuade her. *She certainly takes after me,* I thought.

Caroline's behavior brought to my recollection an incident that occurred a couple of years ago. My good friends who are missionaries were in language school in Central Asia. I was taking care of their boys during the day for several weeks. Four of them…each full of spunk, personality, and an unsanctified sin nature.

Just like me.

Their parents had instructed me that I was to spank for disobedience including "delayed obedience." The inevitable happened and it was time to administer the "rod of discipline," which is not as hostile as it may sound. It was a glue stick, which apparently has taken the lead over the traditional wooden spoon in parenting circles.

Sam had the highest wattage of energy of the four boys. This led to a problem of focusing on completing tasks such as homework or chores before playing. He wanted to do the fun things first and often forgot his priorities. Our personality resemblance was remarkable. This is what led up to my first initiation with the glue stick and our initial bonding of discipline. Sam bent over quietly. His Spider-Man underwear stared up at me unwaveringly from his little rounded bottom. As I swatted his rear end for the first time, tears filled my eyes. Spider-Man melted into a big blob. As if in a foggy distance, his thundering voice shouted at me accusingly from the back of Sam's tush, "You hypocrite!" Looking more closely at Sam's bottom, I could have sworn the masked champion was shaking his fist at me. There was no point in arguing with Sam's hero. I was spanking a six-year-old for the very demon that I struggle with every single day.

Delayed obedience.

Procrastination.

Wanting to do the things *I* want to do first, more than I want to do my daily tasks and disciplines.

After the three swats were over, Sam and I hugged silently for several minutes. Two sinners, in the process of being conformed to His image. There was sweetness in the loving afterwards. We also can experience the Lord's love and compassion after we have had the glue stick administered to our backsides. Sam could have hardened his heart toward me and pulled away in anger and defiance. But he clung to me tightly, allowing me to brush the tears from his eyes. Kindly and gently, he reached up and wiped mine away.

This stands out as a precious memory and reminder that His mercies are even more abundant to me. For I am no different than these children. Just like Caroline, I can be especially sweet and docile when getting my way. And I would rather not face the weakness of procrastination. As much as I would love to hide under the bed from the consequences, there is the inevitable exposure. The Lord loves me enough to bring these deficits and flaws to my attention.

When Jesus called the disciples, they responded immediately. They did not put Him off or spend time *thinking* about obeying. Without hesitation they followed Him. They obeyed instantly. The disciples are our models of how we should respond to His invitations, His leadings, and His promptings. Without questioning or reasoning. From the General Confession in the *Book of Common Prayer*, we find this sacred prayer:

> *Almighty and most merciful Father,*
> *We have erred and strayed from*
> *Thy ways like lost sheep,*
> *We have followed too much the devices and desires*
> *of our own hearts,*
> *We have offended against Thy holy laws,*
> *We have left undone those things*
> *which we ought to have done,*
> *And we have done those things*
> *which we ought not to have done,*
> *But thou, O Lord, have mercy upon us.*

And having prayed those ancient words with a sincere heart, I know there is forgiveness. Sometimes I procrastinate out of fear that I can't accomplish my goals—which is a guarantee that I will not. And many times it is out of habit. This is a pet sin that I have often held close to my heart and caressed and nurtured. I once heard that, "Procrastination is having to deal with the affairs of yesterday." So much of my life has been spent in yesterday that I can't complete what my portion is for today. Although I have taken some steps forward, I am still a long way from where the Lord desires that I be. Proverbs 13:9 says, "A desire accomplished is sweet to the soul." There is contentment and sweetness of satisfaction when we accomplish the promptings of the Holy Spirit and follow His leading.

Procrastinating in obedience to anything the Lord is leading you to do is actually *disobedience*, which is sin. And there will be consequences. I speak with more authority on this subject than I am comfortable with. If you have been under the bed like Caroline, it is safe to come out. Ask for His forgiveness if procrastination is also a weakness in your life. I'm there with you. And He is with us, ever ready to help us in our weaknesses. And if occasionally we need a loving swat like Sam, He does so out of His gracious love. It is the kindness of God that leads our hearts to repentance. A journal from the past contains a prayer I once wrote when He was beginning to show me that this issue was more serious in my life than I realized: *"Father, of all the things in my life that I long for, I pray most that I will cultivate instant obedience to the issues you have spoken to me about. These habits of procrastination are selling my life short of the standard you have for me."*

He doesn't offer condemnation to me, but forgiveness and hope. Thanks be to the One who is never late in His mercy and goodness.

He never procrastinates in His unfailing love.

Traveling Heavy

"The Lord is compassionate and gracious,
slow to anger
and abounding in lovingkindness."
Psalm 103:8, NASB

As often as I have traveled, packing light remains an insurmountable challenge. I just can't seem to get my act together. I always have "too much." Once, just once, I had "not enough." It was on a trip to Romania, which is not the best place to run out of clothes. This traveling tradition of mine has been a constant source of irritation to me and to others as well.

Once on a trip into Ukraine, I packed fairly decently in the area of clothing. Unfortunately, I took an unusual amount of books to prepare for a lecture that I was scheduled to present. One of the men in my group graciously assisted in hauling around my luggage and truly displayed some rather saintly characteristics. But after one long stretch of carrying my multiple bags of paraphernalia, he was notably winded. While resting against a wall, he asked if I would leave my library at home the next time. A legitimate request. That this is an ongoing problem is evidenced by an entry in my journal from three years ago: *"HEAVY. That is what my two suitcases said. In alarming red and white stark letters. The nice man behind the counter looked as if he had herniated something when he picked up my suitcase. I don't know **what** is in those suitcases, but I can **never, never, never** go through this again. I said that last October 22, the last time I flew. But I'm serious. I will never, never, never do this again. **Never.**"*

There have been some trips since then in which I have shown signs of improvement. Unfortunately I have suffered occasional relapses, the most recent one being several months ago. Having finished a nursing assignment in New York, I was flying home on a very early flight which required leaving my hotel at four A.M. The following journal entry torments me in some ways. But in other ways, it is such a tender reminder of His unconditional love:

*This morning was a nightmare. I do not know **what** in the world is in that luggage besides a few clothes and books. In the flurry of checking out, I left my planner at the hotel. Although I have shown much improvement in not losing it since getting a bigger one, today of all days, I would have to leave it. When I discovered that my planner was missing, I thought perhaps I had left it in the car, which meant running back to the parking lot. Because I was weighted down with all of my stuff, I could hardly walk, much less run. My carry-on bag fell open into the parking lot. When I was bending over picking up my bag, the items scattered everywhere, the contents of my purse spilled all over the asphalt. Almost in tears of frustration, I berated myself out loud, **Idiot, Idiot, Idiot!** You are such an idiot. That was all I could say, over and over. As I entered the airport, my name was being paged overhead as the last call for the departing flight. I boarded the plane breathing hard and sweating like a jungle animal. I was disgusted with myself, disappointed, and outdone. And tired. So very, very tired.*

But now I am sitting in First class in a huge and comfortable seat all alone. There is plenty of room in Coach and there was no reason for me to be bumped except that I believe this is an extension of Your grace and mercy. Thank You. Thank You, Father, for Your kindness, compassion, and patience with me. I just pray for Your grace to learn that I cannot carry every book that I want to read. Amen.

As I leaned back in that soft leather seat and rested my head in the pillow of comfort and softness, I had tears in my heart and eyes. It might seem to be a small thing to be bumped into the class of luxury. Whenever it has happened in the past, I have been grateful and enjoyed the experience. But this time it was different. I felt as if the compassion of the Lord was being poured softly over me, penetrating into my tired mind and body. Softly speaking of His love, He wiped away the sting of harsh words that I had spoken against myself. As the flight attendant placed a linen napkin on my lap, I thought of the comparison of His righteousness as fine linen. She served me coffee with real cream, not the powdered imitation that you get in Coach. In First Class, you are made to feel significant and special. That is what I knew the Lord wanted to say to me. He loves me in all my many imperfections. He is patient and compassionate.

That's just the way He is.

Bouquets of Grace

"The Lord will accomplish
what concerns me."
Psalm 138:8a, NASB

A nticipation filled the air as we stood outside the doors of
the church. It was a pleasant Saturday afternoon. My
newly married sister and brother-in-law came out to leave for
their honeymoon, greeted by our clapping and cheering. But
heaven forbid, no wedding would be complete nor departure
appropriate for the "trip to the moon," as I have deemed it,
until the bouquet and garter are tossed.

Shane and Sunnie were like every other blissfully wedded
bride and groom of thirty whole minutes. Because they did not
want to deprive hopeful and optimistic singles in the crowd
the opportunity to experience marital joy, they paused before
their audience. I was especially enjoying my view of this age-old
tradition, as I towered over the heads of all gathered. My five-
foot-nine-inch frame was heightened, having perched myself
on one of Dad's eight-foot ladders. Strategically placed in front
of the glowing couple, I stood prepared. In my right hand, I
held one of Dad's three-foot-wide fishing nets, wrapped in
coordinating ribbon to match the color of our bridesmaid
dresses. Only because of my benevolent heart toward my
younger sister did I let her share my perch. It was about to be
a great moment in our family's history.

Sunnie gently tossed the floral spray. As if in slow motion,
the bouquet arched toward the raised arms of the waiting
maidens. Suspended in the rays of the setting summer sun for
a breath-filled moment, it descended into the hoop of my net

with a tender *whoosh.* Applause and laughter filled the air and I glowed in anticipation. Poor Shawn, my baby sister, did not come away with a bouquet. Just a husband. She met my brother-in-law-to-be in the wedding festivities. He was a groomsman and her appointed escort. In just one short year we were celebrating their wedding. Terribly romantic unless you are the older sister who did not get married. All I had left were some wilted flowers.

Getting married and catching wedding bouquets have absolutely no correlation whatsoever. Having caught at least eighteen, I think I am overqualified to reach that conclusion. There have been some that I have wrestled from the hands of the less fit which I probably should not count.

I no longer stand with all the "wannabe" brides at the "great toss up." This decision was made a couple of weddings ago and enhanced last summer. Having attended the most jubilant wedding of my friends, Bill and Judy, we gathered outside to wish them joy as they began their new life of marital nirvana. Before leaving, they tended to the last important detail of their wedding day: the sacred tradition that would promise certain matrimony to at least two of their single friends. Because of photographs, the ritual hurl was taking place inside, which is precisely why I was standing outside. While waving good-bye to the happy Mr. and Mrs., a friend leaned to me and whispered some chilling words. As she had watched the great throw down, she overheard a rather matronly woman say, "There go all the desperate old maids!"

My eyes rested on the woman she discreetly directed her eyes toward. Although I thought that statement was a bit unfair, not to mention cruel and hateful, I considered overlooking the grave injustice of her words. However, the sting of her words were emblazoned upon my list as one of the most abhorrent and ungracious comments I had ever heard. So what if they were true? I began to make plans to run over her in the parking lot. If unsuccessful, at least to aim for her big toe.

A few weeks later I attended the wedding of another friend. It was marked by the bride, Rosalyn, playing a tambourine as she and Mark marched up the aisle accompanied by the "Hallelujah Chorus." It was a celebration at its finest! The time came for Mr. and Mrs. Medlin to depart for "the moon." The summons to all desperate women was about to take place. And the words of the tactless woman whose big toe I wanted to run over sang out like an out-of-tune tuba in my mind. Making a hasty exit to the front doors, I closed them quietly behind me.

Quickly becoming engaged in conversation with the doorman, I explained why I was hiding. He looked puzzled but said that he would keep the doors closed. From the interior of the large antebellum home, I heard my name being called repeatedly. He saw my look of desperation and tried to help me get off the porch. At that moment, one of my more determined friends found me. "Get in here," she said with clenched teeth. "Don't you want to get married?" There was no negotiating. The kind doorman cast me a pitying look. Feigning a demeanor of grace and dignity, I stood silently with the rest of the giggling females.

"Lord, for the sake of Your Kingdom and my pride, would You please let me catch just one more bouquet? Amen."

Our eyes were glued to the object upon which the outcome of our marital status depended. Up...up...up...it hurtled toward the ceiling. Striking the chandelier with the force of an atomic missile, it was catapulted to the marble floor. There it lay forlornly until it was scooped up by the four-year-old flower girl.

"Okay. That's it. I am out of here. OUT OF HERE."

Turning away in search of the front doors, I heard Rosalyn calling my name. She snatched the bouquet from her niece, who started wailing. Just like I was about to do at any moment.

"Come *back*," she yelled.

Was there no end? Meekly, quietly, I turned back and waited for another dose of humiliation. Again, one of those slow motion moments occurred...the bouquet was coming...coming...straight toward my arms...coming. From my right peripheral vision I saw the hands of another bridesmaid, Ruth, reaching...reaching...reaching...

"Oh no you don't! This baby is MINE!"

With the agile and lithe spring of a young gazelle, I sprang forward in my two-inch heels and secured those sacred rose blossoms in my hands, raising them triumphantly. Sweeeeeet!

Springing back in one swift move, I bounced gently on the balls of my feet. In a split millisecond, I was gazing at the domed ceiling instead of Rosalyn's happy face. My moment of victory turned into a big derriere splat. Walking outside with my prize clenched in my hands, the doorman grinned at me. We exchanged a high five.

Climbing into bed that night and recording the day's events, I looked at the blossoms and smiled. *"Father, my times are in Your hands, my heart and all that it contains. You will accomplish all that concerns me in Your creative way. You are bigger than any number of bouquets, although I am VERY grateful that You let **me** catch this one instead of Ruth."*

I failed to mention that Ruth was using a cane at this time. She could have used it to deflect the bouquet from me, to swat me in the head, or even worse, God forbid, to yank the flowers to herself.

"And thank you for laughter even in the midst of humiliation. And

thank you as well for not letting my dress go flying over my head when I hit the floor, although I haven't even the faintest idea why You let that happen. Thanks again for the flowers. "

With that I hung the perfumed bouquet to the chain of my ceiling fan. And there it remains as a gentle reminder of laughter and sweet things to come.

The Beloved
Bumbling One

"If the Lord delights in a man's way,
He makes his steps firm;
though he stumble, he will not fall,
for the Lord upholds him with His hand."
Psalm 37:23–24, NIV

Stepping onto the stage, I lightly held onto the podium and breathed a sigh of thanksgiving that I remained in an upright position. This may not sound like a great accomplishment for some, but those of us for whom coordination is at times a challenge will appreciate this feat. Whenever I speak before audiences, my initial prayer is simply that I will make it to the podium without any chaos—meaning without falling down. There is sustaining evidence in my life that this is a legitimate prayer request.

Only the night before I had finished scraping some remaining abrasions from my face after carefully soaking my entire face in vitamin E oil. My knees were still a painful testament of an event that had taken place a few days earlier—ironically, just before my speaking engagement for a women's fashion show. I was asked to participate as a speaker and not as a model, which really was quite providential. Models may come in a variety of shapes and sizes, but they all have a few characteristics in common. They are tall, slender, poised, and regal. I am blessed with the first of those characteristics. And only the first. Models glide down runways in upright positions, emanating mystique and charm. They smile alluringly at their audience, who remain captivated by their very presence.

The previous weekend, I had a personal audience of eight very attentive men. I had stopped to visit a friend in her real estate office in North Carolina, and it was my grand exit that prompted the visit of paramedics from Waynesville County. After my visit had concluded, I was gliding out to my car when I unexpectedly stumbled upon nothing else but my own feet. As I was catapulted to the ground, the impact of my body smacked my face to the pavement, jostling my brain, and *worst* of all, leaving my bottom suspended in mid-air. Some sweet lady, whom I couldn't see, stopped to help me dig my face and knees out of the concrete. Later I was to find out that my rescuer was, in fact, a man. Managing to get inside where I dramatically announced that I needed help, I sprawled out on the floor, putting my feet up in a chair before I passed out.

There I was, sprawled on the floor of a real estate office with my legs in the air surrounded by men. To my good fortune, I did have on pants. In my own unique way I was emanating charm and mystique. That is what I keep telling myself anyway. The paramedics that you see on television and those that live in the mountains of North Carolina are quite unrelated. These gentlemen staring down at me were "big pick-um-up truck" kinda boys. The pockets of their Levi jeans bulged with circular containers of that substance that most good men of the mountains love. And some had a familiar pouch of tobacco peeking over the pocket of their T-shirts, which advertised anything from drag racing to shotguns.

After taking my vital signs and putting ice packs on the various bumps and abrasions, I noticed two of the boys bringing in a stretcher.

"Come on Miss Payne—let's take you in to the hospital."

"But I don't *need* to go to the hospital."

"C'mon now. You need to git checked out. Might need to stay for the night."

"Thank you, but I would prefer to sleep in my own bed tonight."

This conversation lasted for several minutes until they realized I was not so bowled over by their charm that I was going to be the submissive type. In silence they stared down at me while occasionally shifting their tobacco around in their mouths. Fortunately, no one spit. Wanting to make them feel useful, I jokingly said, "But I will have a plug of that tobacco." They grinned and one of them spit into an empty Pepsi bottle, I suppose in honor of my request.

"Thank you gentlemen for coming to my rescue. And I am indebted to you for not cutting off my clothes." Having worked in the Emergency Room, I have seen very nice clothes cut to shreds by young paramedics, a bit too eager to try out their new scissors.

One of them beamed sheepishly and kicked the floor with the toe of his boot. "Aw now, I was just reaching for the scissors when you started talking." What I did not say was, "If you had cut my clothes off in front of all these men, it would be *you*, big boy, that would have been sprawled on that stretcher." I just smiled.

As they all trailed out, I sat there talking to the three real estate agents. One of them said, "I think you must have fainted and then hit the ground." Now, for the sake of my dignity, I could have been silent and agreed. But my conscience, as jostled as it was, would not allow me.

"No, I tripped and then fainted. This is just part of my unique charm...it happens every so often. Two months ago at the Presbyterian Church in Charlotte, while walking across the foyer—Splat. The grocery store a few weeks before that.

Slid on a piece of lettuce—Splat. In all honesty, I think I trip on my feet. They are unusually long and I think they just sometimes get in the way." She looked at my feet and her silence indicated that she agreed.

That night as I was soaking in the bath tub, aching all over and trying to get embedded debris out of my knees and face, I broke the silence.

"Lord, is there any particular reason that this sort of thing happens to me with such frequency?" It was an honest question and I wanted an honest answer. Truthfully I was quite discouraged. One disheartening element to this night of affliction was that I had been faithfully working on my ballet videos, the ones that assured me that I would achieve a leaner, stronger, more graceful look without the fear of bulky muscles. Not that for a moment I have ever been afraid of bulky muscles. These exercises are set to classical music and I truly did feel that I was becoming more graceful. I don't mean that I felt I was ready to audition for *Swan Lake*, but I thought I was making progress. Poised and regal, I was emerging in all of my grace and charm. Nothing like an unexpected splat to send me back to the beginner's tape.

I continued to soak in the warm water in silence, and this prayer unexpectedly came into my heart: "Lord, keep me ever mindful of my need of You. I need You. I need You. I desperately need You. For those moments that I am awkward and bumbling and for those moments when I feel inept and I *am* inept, thank You for being greater than all of my falterings. For those rare moments when I actually do appear poised and somewhat sophisticated (until I stand up), although I wish they happened more often, thank You for reminding me that in those moments I need You as much as when I am picking dirt from my teeth. I need You!"

The basic fact of life is that the only thing any of us has any natural talent for, outside of God's gifts and grace, is the ability to fall flat on our faces. Yes, each of us has specific talents and gifts that He has entrusted to us, but none that we can use without Him. Even the most renowned and talented of pagans is unaware that without the most charitable assistance of her Creator, she would never know the applause of the world. Regardless of our family background, education, financial or social status, we *need* Him. We *all* come from the wrong side of the tracks, and He has extended His compassionate hand of grace to us, lifting us when we have fallen, brushing off the dirt, bringing wholeness and restoration to our brokenness.

As I soaked all of my aches and scrapes that night, in answer to my earlier question to the Lord, one of the verses He reminded me of was, "The path of the just is like the shining sun, that shines ever brighter unto the perfect day" (Prov. 4:18). Granted, I would like to walk the path He has before me in an upright stance. Not only physically, but with my mouth, my attitudes, and my daily disciplines. But on those days when I bump and stumble, and on occasion fall, may I remember to fall *forward*. And if one day I find it necessary to start wearing knee pads and crash helmets, at least they now come in fabulous colors. It is fortunate that I had them even just a few days ago when I was bike riding—I made a grand splat. And no, it wasn't a stationary bike. I felt just a slight twinge to my conscience when I rode past someone else piled up on the side of the road. I felt just ever so much better that there was someone else like me.

Though I stumble, I will not fall, for He upholds me with His hand. Perhaps I need to pray that He uses *both* hands!

Confession

"Therefore confess your sins to each other
and pray for each other
so that you may be healed."
James 5:16, NIV

Scenes of the couple flirting seductively with one another flashed across the television screen. Although they were squeezed tightly together on a bench in a flower garden, I had my suspicions that they would soon switch to bedroom furniture. In a matter of moments, they were transported from kissing amidst the petunias to wrestling in tangled sheets.

The Holy Spirit spoke to me, as a father would to his child, in a rather stern tone of voice. "Turn it *off*, Angela."

But I didn't want to. Although I was uncomfortable with what I was seeing, I continued to watch the steamy scene.

"*Now*, Angela." Clicking the television off, I sat there in regret of what I had just exposed my mind and spirit to. It had happened so quickly. I went from flipping through the channels from a documentary on the war in Afghanistan to scenes of lust and sensuality in mere seconds. Drawn like a bug into a sewage drain, I was quickly swept into the downward spiral of immoral thoughts.

Sitting in silence, the Lord continued to speak to me, affirming His calling on my life and to a lifestyle of holiness and purity. This calling is no different than anyone else's, for that is His desire for each of His children. Remembering the verse from James, I knew what I must do. Confess my sin. This event occurred while I was in the home of a dear and godly woman, Betty Watkins. My home was for sale and I was living in her basement while working on a writing project. She was upstairs and I quickly made my way to her.

We sat together and I told her what had just happened. Having already asked the Lord's forgiveness, I prayed and confessed again before Him and now before her. There was forgiveness, cleansing, and renewal. Accountability is such an important tool, available to us to assist in keeping our lives in alignment to His will, like a good check and balance system. In our confession of sins and weaknesses, we can strengthen and pray for one another.

"If we say that we have fellowship with Him, and walk in darkness, we lie and do not practice the truth" (1 John 1:6). By confessing our sins, we transfer them from the darkness of shame and guilt into the light, exposing them as sin. As we confess them to the Father and a trusted friend, we thereby receive cleansing and healing of the breach of holy fellowship that sin causes. Our spirit is willing but our flesh is weak (Matt. 26:41). As long as we try to keep the sin that holds us captive in darkness, we will remain in bondage to it. But as we humble ourselves before God and man, we can walk in the freedom of being captive only of His love.

Whatever the sin is that entangles you—lust, financial chaos, gossip, over-eating, sexual sin, television—bring it into the healing light of truth. There are four trusted friends in my life who help me stay on the path of righteousness. I am quick to call on them when I have erred in the areas in which I am weak. Our individual lists will be different. However, for each of us, our God and Deliverer is the same. He has made provision to set us free from anything that separates us from Him, from anything that is contrary to His nature. Because of His grace, we really can be more committed to His righteousness than we are to sin. Not in our own strength, but in His.

In *The Message,* Eugene Peterson writes: "Sin speaks a dead language that means nothing to you; God speaks your mother tongue, and you hang on every word. You are dead to sin and alive to God. That's what Jesus did. That means you must not give sin a vote in the way you conduct your lives. Don't give it the time of day. Don't even run little errands that are connected with that old way of life. Throw yourselves wholeheartedly and full-time into God's way of doing things. Sin can't tell you how to live. After all, you're not living under the old tyranny any longer. You're living in the freedom of God" (Rom. 6:11–14).

God is encouraging us on to walk in freedom: *though you fall, my precious daughter, you shall not be utterly cast down, for I uphold you with My hand* (Prov. 24:16). There is hope for us, not in ourselves, but in Him. He doesn't offer us condemnation, but grace. Betty exemplified His grace, encouraging me in this walk of holiness. She opened her heart for me to come again if I was tempted so that she might pray with me.

Whatever the sin is that we wrestle with, He has made a way of escape. Satan is relentless in His attempts to wear us down. Be reminded of the truth from Ecclesiastes 4:9–10,12: "Two are better than one, because they have a good return for their work: if one falls down, his friend can help him up. But pity the man who falls and has no one to help him up!…Though one may be overpowered, two can defend themselves. A chord of three strands is not quickly broken" (NIV).

Intertwine yourself with Jesus, first of all, and then with a trusted friend who will speak the truth in love and cover you in prayer and encouragement in your weakness.

There is joy in confession and cleansing. Drink freely of His grace that covers every sin.

You can even ask for refills.

The Sneaky Pounce
Of Aging

"However many years a man may live,
let him enjoy them all."
Ecclesiastes 11:8, NIV

A monumental event occurred in my life about a year ago. I was not prepared for this occasion. The date of the event was looming in the darkening and ominous future. Fear consumed me as I shuddered at the thought of being devoured by the formidable and hideous, yet unseen beast. I heard it hissing, sneering, and encroaching upon me. I was about to plunge into an abyss of utter and complete darkness. The evil date approached me…

My *fortieth* birthday.

Nothing in my journey of life so far has astonished me more than this occasion. And as much as I adore surprises, this was not one that I was savoring. Never have I been so *unprepared* for such a milestone, although you would think that I had forty years to get ready. The remaining "thirty-something" years were so filled with writing deadlines and other major events that I really did not have time to think about the crossing of the "great divide" until just a few weeks before it happened. At that point there was no emotional reserve whatsoever. The sensation that at any moment I might have an emotional seizure would somewhat describe how I was feeling.

Never had I been *so* vintage before—and I was not feeling like a nice bottle of wine that improves with age. In reality, I never really believed that I would turn forty. Not that I was counting on dying before then, but it was one of those events that always happened to people *much* older than I was. In the recesses of my mind, I knew that if and when I ever turned forty, without a doubt, I would be married and have children. That had never been a question. I never imagined that was going to turn out to be an assumption rather than reality. A friend called to assure me that her fortieth birthday was one of her favorites. That would be quite believable. She spent it with her husband in a romantic getaway while leaving her five children at home. *Of course* it was one of the best birthdays of her life! And here I was, quite without a husband or children.

In addition, I was embarrassed. There was a sense of shame. The whispering voices of unseen faces followed me with ruthless intent. "No, she *never* married." "She didn't have children, the poor thing." The imagined conversations were never-ending. Finally I realized that *I'm* not the one who should be embarrassed for not being married. *He,* whoever *he* might be, is the one who should be mortified for taking such an absurd amount of time to find me.

What could I possibly do to assure myself that I was not upset about turning forty, and what could I do to prevent *anyone* from daring to feel sorry or embarrassed for me?

Escape! Flee! Yes! Flee to Paris!

Of course, I would go to Paris and turn forty while swinging from the Eiffel Tower! It was the only resolution to soothe the sting of my affliction while still being in the boundaries of moral and sanctified behavior. After researching fares, I called a couple of friends to see if they were eager in joining me on this birthday extravaganza. They were enthusiastic about dancing with me on the Eiffel Tower until...much to my dismay, I heard that quiet Big Voice that can make you so completely miserable. God has the amazing talent to send an impending sense of misery to those about to go out of His will.

"But Looord," I wailed, "*why* can't I go to Paris?" Back and forth I struggled, wanting *my* way, even having a temper tantrum. Somehow, in my frenzied emotions, I felt His calming peace and assurance that His idea of celebrating my birthday was even bigger than Paris. "You have *got* to be kidding, God...aren't You?" But I was soon to know the sweet and tender touch from my Father. He wanted my birthday to be even more special than I could have planned.

My dear friends Bart and Ginger Combs turned their lovely home into a Parisian cafe and hosted a wonderful party filled with themes of Paris. Loving friends surrounded me. My mother was there, and I found it sweet indeed that she spent that night with me, which was actually the eve of my birthday. Turning to kiss her goodnight, I realized that it was forty years ago that we had started our journey together as she gave birth to me. Somehow it was appropriate to be sleeping together.

We spent the next day together, which will always be a highlighted memory. The following night I concluded the evening of my momentous occasion by turning off the phone and taking a bubble bath by candlelight.

An author has the prerogative to create the details of her book as she desires. It can end triumphantly, romantically, or in tragedy. There is an Author of my life. He knows where to put the entrances and exits of people. He weaves circumstances in such a way that I don't know how I am getting to The End, but I know where the final destination is. My plots are full of surprises and sometimes disappointments. It is a love story of divine romance. Jesus is the author and finisher of my faith (Heb. 12:2).

I might have changed some points of my life outline if God had asked. He did not. All He asked is that I would trust and follow. I truly do not believe that turning forty would have been such an immense event had there been a husband there to hold me and ease me into the transition. No, a husband was not there. But God was. And He will continue to be there, writing my book while turning the pages when a husband is there.

The stories of our lives are of great value. Jesus is writing them. He is the author and finisher of our faith. Our lives are the words to be read by the world around us. May they read of our faith and great joy. And on those pages of disappointments, may they see that our Author wrote the words of life that gave us great comfort, peace, and hope.

Our books are unabridged. Classics. First Editions. And of great value. As we look to "The End" of our life stories, we can be reminded that it is only "The Beginning" of one that goes on forever and ever.

The Red Tutu

*"And my God shall supply
all your need
according to His riches
in glory by Christ Jesus."
Philippians 4:19*

The ballerinas leaped gracefully across the stage in perfect unison and synchrony. Graceful and poised, they smiled gently to their captivated audience. The dancers' movements were fluid, harmonized, and flowing together. Their very presence was graceful and effortless. The accompanying majestic praise music filled the auditorium and the hearts of all who watched. Together they worshiped Him, dancers and audience.

As the performance was concluded, the ballerinas exited together. Their red tutus were shimmering in translucent splendor under the fading lights.

The audience applauded enthusiastically, but none more than a woman behind stage. For not only was she lauding and praising the dancers, she was applauding and praising God.

Barbara Barker, founder and director of Ballet Exaltation, had seen the Lord perform a miracle only a few hours earlier. The same God who once parted the Red Sea for the children of Israel to cross and raised the dead to life was the very same God who had cared enough to send a red tutu to one of her dancers. Since the founding of the classical dance company twenty years ago, she has seen God perform countless miracles as the troupe has danced in worship to the Lord Jesus nationally and internationally.

Who would ever imagine that the God who keeps the universe in order is concerned about a red tutu? Barbara!

Only a few hours before the evening performance, she was unpacking a late shipment of costumes. One, two, three, four, five, six...where was the seventh costume? She began searching hurriedly through the tissue, sure that she had overlooked a tutu. There was none to be found. The color was very distinct, and there was no costume on hand that could be used as a substitute. Quickly praying for the Lord's intervention, she called a local ballet apparel shop and explained the predicament. "Do you have a red tutu in stock?"

The woman on the other end of the line explained that they never carried anything red, just the traditional ballet colors of pink and white. "Wait a minute..." Her voice trailed off.

Barbara held her breath and prayed. The girls had worked so hard and diligently for this very important performance. They must *all* dance!

In a few moments, the woman returned and with the most incredulous tone of voice said, "You are never going to believe this..."

Tucked away in the corner of a closet was one red tutu. The perfect size. The perfect shade of red.

Amazing story. Amazing God.

All tutu the glory of God!

More of You

"Heal me, O Lord,
and I will be healed;
save me and I will be saved,
for You are the One I praise."
Jeremiah 17:14, NIV

My friend Marty Stubblefield has his own tender version of
Little Women. First he married one. Her name is Amy.
Ellie came along four years ago, and Abbie joined them two
years later.

Marty describes the Stubblefield household as just a little
family trying to be faithful and make a little bit of a difference
where they are. They have made a big difference in my life as
I read the stories he loves to write about his family.

"When they were toddlers, my wife spent time teaching my
little ones a bit of sign language. Nothing major, for we don't
know that much. Just a few things to help them communicate
with us. (Ever tried to communicate with a one-year-old?) Amy
taught them the sign for *thank you, please, all done,* and *more.*
She would say the word or phrase and then move their hands
to make the sign. It was really pretty neat watching them learn.

"The sign for *more* is made by putting your fingers and
thumbs together on each hand, where they almost look like a
face. You then place the two hands together where the finger-
tips touch, like the hands are kissing. They softly touch again
and again. This is our sign for *more.*

"One Sunday morning, as we were preparing for church, I
turned on some praise music so that it could be heard

throughout the house. During one particular song, Abbie, my two-year-old, came bouncing into the living room as if she were dancing unto the Lord unashamedly. She was unaware of me quietly singing and lifting up my heart, and also unaware of how cute and funny her little dance looked. She raised her hands in praise while continuing to dance. With her little arms fully extended and her eyes looking toward heaven, she made the *more* sign with her hands. As if to say, 'More…More…More of You, O Lord. More…More…More to You O Lord.'"

Marty went on to share his reaction as he watched his little girl. "My heart jumped and cried out, 'Yes Lord. That is what I want…to give more to You so that I can have more of You. More praise. More worship. More of You. Take all of me so that I may have more of You!'"

Jesus said, "Blessed are ye that hunger for you shall be filled." Sometimes we must ask the Lord to heal and save us from our apathetic hearts that are too full of things or activities. There will be no spiritual hunger and desire for *more* of Him if we are filled with whatever we have allowed to take the place of Him.

My prayer is that each of us may hold our hands and hearts before our Father with the same enthusiasm and eagerness of two year old Abbie. Her child-like joy and love was an extemporaneous expression of her devotion.

May our lives sing daily…More of You, Lord.

Less of Me

More of You.

Thanks to Marty Stubblefield for sharing this story with me.

How the Mind And Body Of a Woman Can Know The Heart of God

Thoughts on emotions, appearances, and finding God in spite of ourselves

Strained Pea
Kind of Day

"The Lord is my helper;
I will not fear."
Hebrews 13:6

The humid air rested upon us like coagulated skimmings from the top of cold chicken broth. Yuck. It was sticky and sultry. Muggy warmth penetrated our cotton clothes.

It was one of the hottest days on the register in Florida and the heat index was off the charts. I was visiting my sister and her family on the day that the air conditioner just happened to have expired.

Sitting in the kitchen, I watched my niece eating her lunch from her high chair. She typically looked like a Gerber baby. But today she had pulverized green peas all over her face and was whiny and uncooperative. My sister, Sunnie, was also in the kitchen. She is quite attractive, in my opinion, but today was …not her best day, shall we say. I will leave it at that.

My brother-in-law came inside, sweating profusely and with a disgusted look on his face. He had been tangling with the air conditioning unit, and I had a suspicion he did not win the battle.

Feeling the need to be quiet and withhold any suggestions or comments, I saved them for my journal that night. *"Everyone thinks that because I am not married, I have grandiose ideas of marital and maternal bliss. I would deny that misjudgment because I know that these strained pea kind of days are part of it."*

Reading back over my journals, I found an entry that made

me smile in remembrance. It was made while I was babysitting for some friends' children. *"Here I sit on a nice fall day with the Fowler children. Lunch was quite domestic today. No over-gushing maternal feelings as potato chips were dumped all over the floor. Andrew smelled of a dirty diaper while Anna was whining and refusing to eat. Rachel spilled her milk twice and Paul was talking incessantly. Smile!"*

Several years ago, my friend Ginger was recounting her day to me. One of the kids had thrown up all over the ceramic tiled floor. As she was cleaning it up, she slipped and almost knocked herself unconscious as her head slammed against the toilet. She said she literally saw stars. Bless her heart, and the hearts of all the other sacrificing mothers who live the daily grind of homework and countless wipe-ups of spilled milk, runny noses, and endless loads of clothes.

I know that one of the desires of my heart is to convey to women the message of not putting their lives on hold while waiting for something better. Some of you might think, "That is exactly what I would like to do! Where is the pause button so I can have just one quiet moment by myself?!"

Hebrews 6:13 tells us that we may say: "The Lord is my helper; I will not fear. What can man do to me?" Perhaps a paraphrased version for mothers should be:

The Lord is my helper;

I will not scream or throw children or things.

*What can my children do to me except make me **think** I am losing my mind?*

God has promised that His grace is sufficient for each season of our lives. For me at present, His grace covers not having children. All of my life I have longed to have five children. At this point, being a 41-year-old non-germinated single woman, you cannot imagine how much I have had to cling to His grace. A journal entry of mine from several years ago gives a small glimpse into this daily walk. *"Yesterday I was involved in a wonderful delivery. A precious couple who loved the Lord and one another. They were delightful. My heart yearns for the day when my legs will be up in the air and I will also be screaming and crying with the pain and joy of childbirth."*

So far the only thing I have done with my legs in the air while screaming in agony is abdominal crunches and leg lifts.

Married friends can look at singles and long for some of the freedoms that they have. Singles can look at their married friends and be wistful about their families. Hebrews 13:5 gives us a recipe for joy that being single or married cannot bring: "Let your conduct be without covetousness; be content with such things as you have." To be content is a choice that we make whether we feel like it or not. When our hearts are overwhelmed with circumstances beyond our control, we can cry out to Him as the psalmist does in Psalm 61. And He will lead us to the Rock that is higher than we are—rescuing us from the turbulence of our discontentment as we reach up to Him. He is our helper through those trying, disappointing, and challenging moments. When we feel overlooked and unappreciated, He understands and is well acquainted with our feelings. He, too, has been overlooked and unappreciated.

And so on those mashed pea kind of days, know that He is near. He appreciates you pouring your life into your children. Jesus had a mother. And He freely expressed His love and gratefulness to her. He knows and understands the unselfish daily walk that you live day in and day out.

He is near on those Gerber, Home Beautiful days as well as on the strained pea ones.

And every day He says to you…"Happy Mother's Day, dear daughter of mine."

His Lovingkindness

"Because Your lovingkindness is better than life,
my lips shall praise You.
Thus I will bless You while I live;
I will lift up my hands in Your name."
Psalm 63:3–4

Racing down the halls of the hospital, I felt that familiar sense of being overwhelmed—similar to tripping into an open sewage drain and not knowing how to swim. Not only was work particularly challenging that day; several other trying events of my life seemed to be pursuing me. Life at the time was difficult, without exaggeration. A hospital staff member whom I hadn't seen in a while approached me and smiled.

"Hi Angela! How are you?" I knew that if I told her the truth, she would be convinced I was on the brink of a psychotic snap and in danger of breaking into the anesthesia cart and sniffing the contents. Pausing for one of those eternal moments, I silently shrieked a simple prayer to the Lord. Only to God can you shriek and no one else hears. The old classic stand-by— that freeze-dried, canned response—was on the tip of my pursed lips. This answer has made astonishing liars out of most of us: *"Fine."*

For most of my life I have done quite well with the proper response, *"I'm fine thank you. And how are you?"* However, I was confident that if I said it on this day, I would choke on my insincere words and most likely convulse and contort as well as do other unladylike things.

For some undefined reason, I wanted to answer the question honestly, without emotionally throwing up all over her and thus frightening her out of her polite wits. The following words came out of my mouth: "Life is good! Life is hard but life is good!"

Pausing in the hallway, I *heard* what I had just said. My whole attitude about my circumstances changed in an incredible way. I didn't have to be someone comparable with the ranks of Einstein to figure out that life is sometimes challenging. Even at its best, life can still be like a good kick to the internal organs. *But,* life in and of itself is fabulous. In the movie *Life Is Beautiful,* Italian filmmaker Roberto Benigni illustrates the premise that even in the difficult and pain-filled moments of our lives, we can notice and savor life's beauty.

My perception gauge of God's goodness was in need of an adjustment. I was walking. And breathing. I could pick up items with my two hands. I was not paralyzed. I could go to the bathroom on my own without assistance or dialysis. I was not starving or in a war-torn country. I could send money to those who were in starving and war-torn nations. And I could go myself if He so led. I have the joy of knowing that life in Christ is eternal life and we say good-bye only for a season.

In spite of my being bent out of shape, God was and is and will always be in control. And He can bend me anyway He wants to. For He is a good and wise God. His lovingkindness is better than life itself. In the best of times and the worst of times.

A Lesson
In Gratefulness

*"Through Jesus, therefore,
let us continually offer to God a sacrifice of praise—
the fruit of lips that confess His name."
Heb 13:15, NIV*

While getting into my car one night after shopping at the grocery store, my attention was drawn to the corner of the parking lot. Two men had made a shelter on one side and were huddled around a fire. Quickly walking back into the store, I spent the next several minutes happily gathering food items that I thought these men would enjoy. Being careful to choose "man food," I made sure none of the items contained ingredients such as whole wheat, tofu, or soybean oil.

Having completed my purchases, I walked toward them. Approaching them smiling, I just knew they were going to be so happy and grateful for some nice food for dinner. Introducing myself to them, I held out the sack full of groceries. They looked at me with disdainful, nonchalant interest.

"We don't need food, just money." They didn't even say thank you. Outraged at their ungratefulness, I stomped away. As I was driving home, stewing over their response, I heard the Lord say (when I finally got quiet enough to listen), "Hey, hey, HEY! Now why are you in such a huff? Angela, you do the same thing. Daily. Consistently. And you have been doing it all your life."

There was silence the rest of the way home.

As I continued to drive home in subdued reflection, I

remembered a prayer that I had once read: "Thou that hast given so much to me, give one thing more—a grateful heart." I was reminded of the countless times when I have not felt grateful for the many dear gifts God has so graciously blessed me with. The knowledge or memory of those gifts fade all too quickly when I am hurting or feeling the disappointment of dreams dashed or fading. If at any time I become focused on what I *don't* have, I find it impossible to have a grateful heart.

But the Giver of life and the gracious Giver of every good and perfect gift does not ask us to give thanks only when we feel like it. We are instructed to give thanks in *all* circumstances. As we offer our thanksgiving to Him, we acknowledge our trust in Him. In essence, we are praising Him for His goodness and faithfulness. "It is good to give thanks to the Lord, and to sing praises to Your name, O Most High; To declare Your lovingkindness in the morning, and Your faithfulness every night" (Psalm 92:1–2).

Thanksgiving and praise have a way of squeezing out negative disappointments. They keep our hearts free of bitterness and offending attitudes. Just as children must be taught to say "thank you," we too sometimes need to have our response of thanksgiving cultivated. Thus our reaction to situations, whether challenging or enjoyable, will be one of gratefulness. We will recognize that every good and perfect gift is from God.

Let us give thanks in all things. Consider some of the "150 Overlooked Blessings" that Sarah Ban Breathnach lists in her book, *Simple Abundance: A Daybook of Comfort and Joy.* This is a tool she designed for women to begin to shift toward an attitude of gratefulness.

Her blessings include:

An afternoon to do as you please.
A walk in the woods and becoming aware
 of life all around you.
Two hours in a wonderful bookstore.
Delighting in other people's children.
Trying something new and loving it.
That moment of relief when you feel the pain has subsided.
Answered prayers.
The warmth and security of home.
Crossing the threshold and closing the door after a
 hard day.
Letting go gracefully without regrets.
Having a congenial conversation with a stranger on a plane,
 train, or bus.
Hearing a piece of music that instantly touches your soul.
Reading a passage in a book or a poem that expresses
 exactly how you feel.
The sacred release of a good cry.
Holding hands.
Being upgraded to first class.
Seeing him and having your heart skip a beat.
Seeing him and finally feeling nothing (!).
Having your child appreciate your sense of humor.
Receiving a love letter. Writing one.

Her ongoing list is refreshing and a joy to read. She helps to arouse in us the ability to see the many simple and abundant joys in our daily lives. Each of our lives is composed of innocent and precious delights. I encourage you to take note and make your own list of things for which you are thankful. Begin like the poet George Herbert did: "Thou that hast given so much to me, give one thing more—a grateful heart."

How Does
He Love Me?

*"How great is the love the Father has lavished on us,
that we should be called children of God!
And that is what we are!"*
1 John 3:1, NIV

*Winnie the Pooh was sitting in his house
one day, counting his pots of honey,
when there came a knock on the door.
"Fourteen," said Pooh. "Come in.
Fourteen. Or was it fifteen?
Bother. That's muddled me."*

—*A. A. Milne*, The House at Pooh Corner

My heart is gracious toward the beloved character of Pooh, probably because I am so much like the little round bear. Details sometimes cause me to be absolutely befuddled. And like dear Pooh, all I can say is, *Bother. That's muddled me.*

It never fails when I drive into a gas station that I do one or all three of the following: Pull the lever that opens my trunk instead of my gas tank. Pull up too far and have to back up to reach the tank. Pull to the wrong side of the tank. (Even when I have a car for several years, it has been a challenge to remember this somewhat elusive detail.)

One of the characteristics I would like in a husband is that he would keep my car filled with gas. Surely you can understand why this desire is so important to me. Actually, having to do it myself is one of the things that enhances my prayer life. Because I so dislike putting gas in my car, I spend a great deal of time driving on fumes and prayer.

Another detail that befuddles me is setting the table. If I go for even a week without setting a table, I truly am muddled when it comes to remembering on which side of the plate the silverware goes. As much as I love to cook and entertain for others, I usually whip up a protein drink for myself or eat yogurt out of the carton, which does not require a formal setting. Yes, I know how to set a table properly, but sometimes I have to pause for a very long moment and consider how it is done.

In recent years there has been talk of the right and left side of the brain. Even at this moment I can't remember which side functions in a specific capacity. While recently in a bookstore to buy a book about drawing with the brain's right side, I asked for the book about drawing with the left side of the brain. Or was it the right...?

As far as following directions on a map...you can forget me trying to figure out all those squiggly lines. A highlighted Trip Tik from AAA is best to avert traveling disasters.

There are enough deficits in my life that I could indeed spend a great amount of time dwelling on them. Too much time has been wasted berating myself for weaknesses and failures. Saying very unkind things about myself one morning, while running out the door late for work, the thought occurred to me: "You know, Angela, you would be so hurt and offended if anyone else said those things about you or someone you love." The realization of the Father's love for me prompted me to write in my journal that night a spin-off from Elizabeth Barrett Browning: *How does He love me, let me count the ways.* I began to list some of the ways the Lord loves me.

He loves my love for flowers,
    for He made them for me to enjoy.
He loves to hear me laugh—especially when I am alone.
He loves my naturally curly hair—even when I used to iron it.
He loves me when I am fifteen pounds overweight.
He loves me when I lose my temper.
He loves me when I am sleeping.
He loves me when I oversleep.
He loves me when I am silent
    before a big fat moon and remember that He made it.
He loves to see me dance alone.
He loves me when I run around in circles
    and feel like a complete moron.

He loves me! He loves me! He loves me!!!!
Exclamation point ad infinitum!
He loves me through all of my multitude of imperfections.
He is cheering and applauding me on. He is crazy about me!

Like Pooh, I probably will continue to get muddled and dizzy about simple decisions. But most of all, I am secure in His unconditional love for me. Just as we take joy in watching our children play when they are not aware of our observation, so it is with Him. He delights in us when we aren't even thinking of ways to please Him. He says to me as a tender Father, "Behold what manner of love I have bestowed on you—you are a child of God!" Yes, there is a higher standard that He desires for me in areas of weakness. And just because He loves me, He will continue to bring these deficits to my attention. He doesn't do it as a harsh father. His eyes are compassionate and filled with grace, even when my own vision is blurred because I am focusing on my flaws.

If you have those days when you are like Pooh—muddled and befuddled—remember these loving words:

> *"The Lord your God in your midst,*
> *the Mighty One, will save;*
> *He will rejoice over you with gladness;*
> *He will quiet you with His love,*
> *He will rejoice over you with singing."*
> *Zephaniah 3:17*

He sings a love song over you, His beloved one.

Going Postal

"Consider it a sheer gift, friends,
when tests and challenges come at you from all sides.
You know that under pressure,
your faith-life is forced into the open
and shows its true colors.
So don't try to get out of anything prematurely.
Let it do its work
so you become mature and well developed,
not deficient in any way."
James 1:2–4, The Message

Some days I am like a slow-moving river. Peaceful. Easygoing. Coming upon a rock or log, I can flow over and around it with ease, grace, and harmony of the elements, producing a sweet melodious river song. But some other days the slightest detour in my flow of life can produce a torrent of emotions comparable to the Colorado River Rapids and similar to an erupting sewage geyser. Those are the days I feel I should hand over my car keys and take up broom riding. As much as I would like to dress it up, cover it up, blame it, or ignore it, I have a temper. And sometimes the temper has me. When I am led by my temper instead of the Holy Spirit, I can allow it to do strange things with me, through me, and to me.

Yes, I can be very kind and tender. Not to forget gracious. And even saintly and tolerant.

And also rude and obnoxious and overbearing and hateful. Just to name a few qualities that always arrive at the most unexpected moments, like a straight-line wind on a spring day.

Let me illustrate my point. A few summers ago I had a very

important package to mail. Calling ahead to the post office, I verified their closing time and arrived with a few minutes to spare. As I turned the handle to go inside...I found it locked. Dead bolted. "Blast it all!" I muttered. It had taken me twenty extra minutes in rush hour traffic, and I had still arrived on time, or so I thought. Now I was standing outside a padlocked door of the United States Post Office at 4:57 p.m. Banging on the metal door several times, I hoped someone would come.

Silence.

It wasn't tranquil quietness. Just irritating.

It was also one of the hottest days of the summer and my emotional temperature was soaring. My manic gauge suddenly went into overload as I heard the bells and whistles sounding off in my brain, similar to the horns of distress on a sinking ship. Frantically, I looked for a place to take cover from the inevitable chaos that would occur unless I veered from this course of destruction. The restraining lid burst from the fermenting pressure and began spewing. Bellowing a frustrated shriek, I pulled back my size twelve shoe and kicked the door. Hard.

Absorbing the pain of my throbbing toe, I barely glanced up when a postal worker came from the side of the building.

"I'm sorry I kicked your door."

"Didn't hurt me and won't hurt it," he said nonchalantly. "It's a metal door—solid metal."

He looked at me without saying another word and walked away shaking his head.

There truly are times that I would like to hide from myself. It's difficult to address weaknesses I would rather not face. But one of the many cries of my heart is, "Father, don't leave me like I am. Out of your grace and mercy, continue to allow me to see these areas. Even if it is embarrassing."

We really must take responsibility when we fly off the handle in anger, whether at a metal door or with people. The postal worker was absolutely right. I did not hurt that door when I kicked it. Just my big toe. But what of the times when I have erupted with my mouth? Words spew out that are hot and volatile. Words laced in sarcasm. Words that cannot be retrieved. My toe healed after that particular eruption. But emotional wounds are not so quick to heal. In my journey thus far, God has encouraged me, prompted me, and on occasion, made me completely miserable until I have asked forgiveness for spouting off or raising my voice disrespectfully at someone.

I'm not talking about agreeing or disagreeing with someone. For certainly there will always be a multitude of conflicting viewpoints on any number of issues when people are involved. Political and denominational differences exist, and varied opinions within families and friendships. Or for some extremists, perhaps a conflict with the United States Post Office. And yes, there are times when discussions, viewpoints, and disagreements can be verbalized. But each can be done with honor and respect to one another's differences.

This journey is an ongoing testament of grace in my life. Many months before our security system tightened up at airports, I felt as if the woman checking my luggage was trying to provoke me and being ever so obnoxious. That was not my problem. But when I reacted to and against her authority, I allowed what I perceived as a control issue for her to become *my* problem. When I was finally through the checkpoint, getting ready to board, I knew that I had to go back to her and clear my conscience. The Holy Spirit can be most unrelenting when necessary.

"Ma'am, I just needed to come back and apologize for getting upset with you."

She was taken aback and appeared embarrassed. "Oh, that's okay. Everybody has a bad day now and then."

"But as a Christian, I must and want to ask your forgiveness for my impatience."

She smiled awkwardly and thanked me for coming back. We clasped hands warmly and I walked away forgiven.

Whenever I raise my voice in frustration at anyone, especially a family member, I am prompted to go back and ask forgiveness. Not necessarily for the words, but for the spirit in which they were spoken. The humility of the One who has forgiven us demands that we follow His example. Jesus doesn't yell at us in frustration when we fail and miss the mark. He is not haughty or proud or boastful.

We can be so proud of our goodness, boastful of our humility, and haughty about our accomplishments. We are *foolish* if we ever lose sight of the fact that there is no good thing in us that He has not put there by His grace.

As confirmation of His grace and my progress, the same postal scenario occurred recently. It was hot. I had several minutes to spare, and the door was locked. Like a sane person, I turned around and got into my car and drove home sweetly... with all ten toes intact. Talk about amazing grace!

Swimming in Grace

"You shall love the Lord your God
with all your heart, with all your soul,
and with all your strength."
Deuteronomy 6:5

"**O**h, Sissy! You look bee-U-tiful!"
"Caroline, I wish that men had the unusual appreciation for allure and loveliness that you have."

She was enthusiastically sincere in her five-year-old affirmation, and my fragile self-esteem needed all the help it could get. I was in this predicament because I will *almost* go to the ends of the earth to bring joy to my nieces and nephews. We were on vacation in the mountains during the winter. Caroline wanted to go swimming in the heated pool along with my other niece, Lydia. Not having my swimsuit with me, I had resorted to going to Wal-Mart to get something suitable for the event. Jacqueline Kennedy, Katherine Hepburn, and all Gap models look stunning in those little numbers similar to shorts and halters. To my surprise, the Wal-Mart department for swimwear apparel contained quite an impressive inventory.

Confidently breezing past their matronly one-pieces, Caroline and I gathered several of the cuter mix-and-match suits. It had been a couple of years since I had purchased a new swimsuit, and I was actually beginning to enjoy this shopping adventure. This was my attitude until I walked into the dressing room. My state of optimism was about to be wrenched cruelly from me. For prior to trying on one of those adorable little numbers, I was very sincere in my belief that I was *just a few* pounds overweight. You know…*winter weight.* Silly of me to think spandex could cover what were actually my pounds of denial.

Choosing bright colors was a good move, or so I thought. A distraction. As we were cramped into a rather minuscule dressing room, the only expanse of substantial size was my rear end, which was reflected in the three full-length mirrors. My neon spandex was glaring at me with brutal honesty. I murmured that if we were at a competing department store, I could be their Blue Light Special. Not for swimsuits mind you, but for Slim Fast. It was a dismal thought and I was in a state of despair. Melancholy, gloom, and hopelessness managed to squeeze into the dressing room with us, though I don't know how they fit. I was not having a bad hair day. It looked cute. It was a *Bad Backside Day.*

"Caroline, are you *sure* you want to go swimming?" Her undaunted enthusiasm for this aquatic adventure was reflected as she squealed and jumped up and down. How do you say no to an innocent and enthusiastic child who loves you unconditionally despite your taut spandex?

"When I grow up, I want to look just like you, Sissy," she lisped. My heart melted, but unfortunately not my rear end.

As we headed to the check out line, she found what she obviously thought was the perfect accessory to my outfit: a fluorescent pink see-through lace cover up to go over my chartreuse and blue derriere.

"No, sweetie, we are already going to have to pass out Dramamine if I do any fast moves. This is enough damage for one day."

Fortunately few people were in the pool. Dropping my towel, I bounded into the warm water with the speed, dexterity, and agility of a sand crab. And for two wonderful hours I was safe. Covered. Surrounded. Protected.

And I might add, having a most wonderful time with my two nieces. Ironically, Lydia was initially scared to come into the water while I was terrified to come out.

Recently I was walking on the beach in Canada. What caught my attention even more than the lovely beach was the number of women, of all shapes and sizes, savoring the sun. They weren't obsessed with what they looked like. I should move there. Now, maybe those women weren't crazy about the size of their thighs. Perhaps they were working on their diets and exercises. But for the moment, they were inviting the sun to soak into their skin, not hiding in a beach towel like I would have been. I'm not yet there. But I hope I am headed in that direction.

Have you been there? Inhibited and ashamed of your outward appearance in any way? Of course you have. You are a woman! And if you are like me, you have to quickly remind yourself that God is concerned about the dimensions of your heart much more than the dimensions of your thighs.

Paul speaks of having an enlarged heart (2 Cor. 6:11). How do I get a heart that is broader than my thighs? By following the first commandment that He gave to us. To love Him with all our hearts and souls. To love Him and His truths more than I love *me*. But when I start concentrating more on my appearance than on my heart and my relationship with Him, the only things that remain large are my thighs and all that is connected to them. And that is a dismal thought indeed.

Two Types of People

"Godliness with contentment
is great gain. "
1 Timothy 6:6

My eyes gazed unseeingly out of the small window of the airplane. The voice of the captain diverted my thoughts from a place far away geographically, but so dear to me that it had taken residence in my heart. I had just left there—the former Soviet Union. A group composed of multi-church denominations made the trip together. The purpose was to bring Bibles to the Christians there and to have the opportunity to meet many of these believers. It had been a wonderful trip with so many prayers answered and doors of opportunity miraculously opened to us.

The Lord had provoked my heart in ways I had not expected—stretching and bringing me to a new level of surrender to His plans and purposes. At present, I was subdued and not really in a mood for talking. The woman in an adjoining seat interrupted my thoughts. She was striking in her appearance—polished and sophisticated. Her manner was poised. She exuded confidence as she sipped her cocktail.

She had come aboard when we stopped in Germany to change planes. After an exchange of pleasantries, I learned that she worked for the American Embassy. She asked where I had traveled and seemed to be interested in my experiences.

"Tell me about the people in Russia," she gushed. "Are they happy?" Her "happy" took about four syllables to come out of her pretty and meticulously outlined lips.

Countless precious faces raced through my mind as I

remembered their stories and lives, the sweet children and humble homes. Revisiting their modest surroundings in my mind, I recalled their contented and grateful hearts.

Turning to my impeccably dressed and polished travel companion, who was peering at me over the rim of her martini, I quietly spoke. "There are two types of people in Russia. Many live day to day without hope, only despair and depression. There is no happiness. But there are others who have a measure of contentment and joy that most likely you and I have never known. You see, their joy is from the eternal hope found in their relationship with Jesus Christ. It is not based on their circumstances. There is nothing in their physical surroundings that is conducive to happiness...only in their relationship with Jesus."

She sat there with her cocktail suspended for a moment and then was silent for the rest of the trip.

We both were. Pulling out my journal, I wanted to spill out all of the questions and turmoil that I felt. My spirit was deeply troubled. Not even so much by what I had been exposed to in Russia, but by what I had seen in my own heart.

"Father," I prayed, "how am I supposed to feel about my life in comparison with those dear believers we left behind in Russia? Guilty? Should I give all of my nice things away? Do you not want me to have pleasant and comfortable surroundings?"

While continuing to pray on the plane, I heard the Lord say to me, "Angela, it's not the *things* that are so important." At that moment, I could envision all of my earthly treasures in my hands. My palms were open and flat.

Unclenched.

"Your hand is to stay open around these things, Angela, never grasping or clutching them tightly."

I felt as if He were saying, "I am not requiring that you give up 'things' at present, but to be grateful for them." And if at any point, He asks me to release them, then I pray that I will do it with joy. For when we start clutching at anything, whether it is in relationships or tangible, physical things, our heart of gratitude becomes one of possessiveness. If our identity is gained from our things and is greater than our identity with our Savior and our walk with Him, something is amiss.

A prayer I once heard someone pray goes along with my heart cry:

"Lord, make me more thankful and more generous.
May I be less attached to and in love with things,
and more attached to and in love with You
and the souls made in your image."

Amen.

Taming of the Shrew

"Fret not thyself."
Psalm 37:1, KJV

It was a lovely spring morning. Most people's mood and dis-position are enhanced at this happy season. Who can be in a negative frame of mind when the daffodils are blooming? Or when young, fresh hostas are peeping up from the earth, just waking after a long winter's sleep? Those are the sort of days that make me want to roll around in the dirt, curl up in a ball, and sleep in the sun—sort of like my basset hound.

But not this particular morning. To this day, I cannot remember what prompted such a hellatious funk. *Yeoua!* Indian feathers and war paint would have been appropriate attire. For those who know me, you are suspicious that I had not had coffee. Incorrect assumption. My outlook on living had nothing to do with a caffeine deficit. No, I had partaken of my usual quota of three cups.

There is a Yiddish word that described me all too well: *kvetching.* It is defined as one who nags—one who is known to be shrewish, whining, muttering, and scowling. A grouch.

That would have been an accurate description of me on that fresh spring morning. All of the above. Nothing was going as planned and I vented my frustration out loud. Although there was no one to listen to me, I ranted and raved with all the drama of an impassioned actress. I spared nothing but hissing and foaming at the mouth. The thought was floating around in the recesses of my mind, "*If* you were married and acting this way, there would only be one solution. The undeserving and dear man would have to fill a tub with water, his only option being to hold your head under until you were silent."

That imagery was enough to make me laugh and pull myself out of my emotional demise. It also made me pause, acknowledge my need for God's grace, and ask forgiveness for allowing myself to get into that state. Some women might defend my *kvetching* mood by championing the cause for out-of-kilter hormones. No dearies. Whatever the levels of our estrogen, even if it is off the chart, we are still instructed to "fret not."

We don't have the liberty of allowing ourselves to be in a "state of vexation," which is how Webster's defines *fretting*. Some women I know use the age-old hormonal excuse for cantankerous attitudes at *least* three weeks out of the month! During those days that hormones are plummeting, or when they are accelerating, our responses can still be guided by God's grace and led by the Holy Spirit. He will make a way of escape when we are tempted to react in frustration or anger (1 Cor. 10:13).

Oswald Chambers shared his thoughts about fretting in *My Utmost for His Highest*: "Fretting always ends in sin. We imagine that a little anxiety and worry are an indication of how really wise we are; it is really more an indication of how wicked we are. Fretting springs from a determination to get our own way."

Whether we are fretting because we are anxious about the outcome of circumstances, or simply because we are in a bad mood, we must ask forgiveness for our fretful minds and actions. For being a shrew instead of a sweetheart. We have taken our focus from His adequate grace and put it upon ourselves, our feelings, and our circumstances. If we base our lives on emotions or the details of our surroundings, we will falter and fail every time.

My brother-in-law, Brian, interprets "fret not" as "freak not!"

Why do we get freaked or spooked at the thought of relinquishing our mood swings or trusting God fully? Is it because we would rather control our lives than depend upon Him? It is inconsistent with our faith, but at times we are more comfortable worrying than trusting. The Lord is ever so willing to subdue our clamoring emotions and our fretting hearts. And those around you are always *most* appreciative when He does!

Or if all else fails…there is always the bathtub!

I Told You So

*"There is therefore now no condemnation
to those who are in Christ Jesus."*
Romans 8:1

Falling face forward into a cold creek bed was not what I had in mind on a winter outing with my young nieces and nephew. Their piercing shrieks filled the air as I tried to dig myself out of the creek bed. Jumping up and down, they exclaimed, "Sissy fell in the creek! Sissy fell in the creek! Oh noooooo!"

Everyone was home for the holidays, and I had taken Caroline, Lydia, and James Luke for a walk on our country road. We had stopped at the bridge to throw rocks and leaves into the rapid stream. Because of a dam the beavers had built, our leaves would not float. My idea was to loosen the dam so that the water would flow downstream. Making my way toward the bank, I carefully maneuvered myself toward the water so that I could push the biggest log away. All three children watched silently, except for seven-year-old Caroline, who said at least four times, "Sissy, you should go to the other side." Ignoring her, I continued to try and loosen the log. That is when I slipped. With a bellow similar to a Beluga whale, my full body length indented the water. It just happened to be the coldest day registered that winter. The icy water saturated my layers of clothing and penetrated my skin. With my teeth rattling together and my lips turning blue, Caroline called out from her perch on the bridge above me, "I *told* you to go to the other side." Lydia, who is the little echo of her older cousin, lisped, "You *should* have gone to the other side, Sissy!"

James Luke peered over the edge of the bridge and waved to his leaf now floating down the creek. "Bye, bye!" he called cheerily. My two-year-old nephew tottered eagerly to pick up more leaves and rocks. Standing there as a shivering and dripping mess, I was somewhat warmed by his happy face.

As we made our way home, Caroline continued to remind me that I should have gone to the other side, speaking with all the authority of her second grade wisdom. That is until I threatened to use her to dam up the creek again if she reminded me just one more time.

In a matter of moments, I was in a warm shower. Caroline's words did not bother me so much as what they reminded me of. My memory was stimulated to the many times I have been presented with the opportunity to say, "I told you to do it *my* way." Someone did not heed my wise counsel and fell. Did I help them up with graciousness and kindness? Did I offer them a warm shower or a hot drink? Or did I just leave them there in the elements because I was so exasperated with them? What would Jesus do? Breathe a sigh of disapproval or convey a look expressing His displeasure?

My estimation is that women respond this way more than men. We have such a natural way of expressing our true feelings—"humph," or a subtle snort seems to be quite popular. I sincerely doubt that Jesus ever rolled His eyes at those who had made mistakes, nor did He make subtle gestures of displeasure. He was the essence of Colossians 3:12: "Therefore, as God's chosen people, holy and dearly loved, clothe yourselves with compassion, kindness, humility, gentleness, and patience" (NIV). Those are the characteristics that we are to wear. Any article of spiritual clothing labeled "condemnation or judgment" should be yanked faster than a pair of spandex pants after Christmas. It is out of place—it doesn't look proper. In fact it looks terribly unattractive.

In *Women of a Generous Spirit,* Lois Mowday Rabey writes, "Women of a generous spirit hold back judgment. Grace gives people a place to make mistakes. Attitudes of grace give others room to relate with God personally and apply His truth in their lives as they discern His leading. Givers of grace also recognize that they themselves are not infallible—they can make mistakes in judgment and misunderstanding the hearts of other brothers and sisters in Christ."

Let me underscore and highlight Rabey's last point: "*Givers of grace recognize that they themselves are not infallible—they can make mistakes in judgment and misunderstanding the hearts of other brothers and sisters in Christ.*"

Yes, girls, it is indeed true, believe it or not! How quick we are to assume someone has made a mistake because they did not follow *our* advice. We make judgments upon innocent people without full understanding. That we take this responsibility upon ourselves is quite a phenomenon. *Why do we do this?* Pardon my subtlety, but most of the time it is *none of our business.* There will be circumstances of others' lives that we will never understand nor were we meant to. Our criticism and speculation can create a great deal of hurt that could so easily be avoided. Let's be slow to offer our advice and condemnation and as quick to extend grace to others as He does to us.

Be an Extravagant Giver of Grace.

A Kid's Take on Stress

"Cast your burden on the Lord,
and He shall sustain you;
He shall never permit the righteous to be moved."
Psalm 55:22

Children often see life from a less-muddled perspective than adults. Perhaps it's because they usually have their faces turned upward. Even sunflowers are most glorious in splendor when they lift their lovely faces toward the rays of sunlight. Is it true that as adults we are sometimes more intent upon looking at our planners, computers, or palm organizers than turning our gaze toward a heavenly perspective?

We would be wise to broaden our perspectives to include observations of life through a child's eyes. Recently, I had a conversation with one of my ten-year-old friends. We were talking about one of our favorite book series, *Anne of Green Gables*. Mary Beth was reading L. M. Montgomery's works for the first time. Observing her delight in reading prompted warm memories of my discoveries in literature at that age. Her reluctance to put her book down for even a few minutes to eat dinner reminded me of a time when I would rather read than eat.

Our conversation led to the topic of adulthood. Mary Beth assured me that she wouldn't mind staying ten all of her life so that she could read as much as she wanted. She explained that grown-ups are just *too* stressed to take out time from their busy schedules to read. Interested in knowing what she would recommend for adults, I asked her to write down some tips. A few hours later she handed me her thoughts, which I found to be well worth thinking about.

10 Tips for Stressed Grown-Ups
From a Kid

1. You know how you are always running to and fro?
Take a break.
2. You know when your bones hurt? It's because of standing
up a lot. Sit down once in a while.
3. Do not stress out about being fat. I mean, you got to look
good but don't go overboard. You look good if you are
in the Lord's path.
4. *Please* don't stress out about football. It's just a *fun* game.
5. Money, yeah, you need a lot of it, but don't worry if you are
doing bad. You will get back on track.
6. Wrinkles aren't that bad. As parents say, "it doesn't even
show!"
7. Don't stress out about small stuff.
8. Take a nap!
9. Eat all you want once in a while.
10. Don't worry about getting old. You can always be young
in your heart and can always have fun!

Well said, Mary Beth! Who would deny that our society has
become addicted to stress and over-commitment? Richard
Foster, in his book *Freedom of Simplicity*, writes, "In contempo-
rary society, our adversary majors in three things: noise, hurry,
and crowds. If he can keep us engaged and in 'muchness and
manyness,' he will rest satisfied!"

Our culture is on the quest to "de-stress" as evidenced by a
new market in candles, bubbles, lotions, oils, and mud packs
to assist in promoting relaxation. We have music to soothe
frayed nerves while bringing calmness and tranquility, herbs
and vitamins to protect us from stress, and even potions with

special atomizers to spray on our sheets to enhance our sleeping. We can soak in bubbles all day and even drink relaxation by the bottle. But if there is not quietness in our hearts, we are simply touching the peripheral issue. It is only when we are quiet and still within our hearts and free of cluttering noises that God can reach that deeper place within us.

God wants to soothe our furrowed brows and bring tranquility to our hearts. He says, *Come to me all you who are weary and weighted down. Let me take from you the burdens that you are not supposed to be carrying. Connect with Me, so that you can be strengthened to fulfill the tasks I have appointed to you and not the ones that others have tried to place on you. For I have not equipped you to carry their obligations or responsibilities.*

We may be stressed because of a planner that is bulging, pants that are too tight, wrinkles that have turned to crevices, or a bank account that seems to be depleted more often than sufficient. Jesus wants to take our frustrations and fears from us if we will let go. He instructs us to cast our cares upon Him because He cares for us (1 Peter 5:7).

There have been countless times when I have named out loud whatever anxious thought or frustration was tugging and relentlessly pounding upon me. "Father, not only do I cast this at your feet, I throw, hurl, and heave it upon You. It is too heavy. I cannot try to carry it any longer. Forgive me for taking the extra weight upon me."

At times, arduous circumstances may come upon us through no fault of our own such as with sickness or the sudden loss of a job or a loved one. We cannot delete those things from our planners. Then we must throw the emotional weight upon Him and believe that His grace is sufficient not only for the seconds and hours that make up the days. His arms are wide to receive whatever He needs to take from us. My ten-year-old friend had some good words for us that parallel the words of Jesus when He said, "Do not worry about your life" (Matt. 6:25). You mean we really *can* relax and trust that He is in control?

Mary Beth said so. And I think she is a pretty smart kid.

Thanks to Mary Beth Watkins for her tips on improving our adult quality of life.

The Ethical Virgin

*"There is a generation that is pure in its own eyes,
yet is not washed from its filthiness."*
Proverbs 30:12

Recently I completed a course on Ethics and Christianity at a local university. The notes I took in class were meaningless in comparison to the revelation I had about myself. During a lecture, the question was proposed by the professor, "If there were no God, would you live your lives differently?" My mental list was quickly filling up with all the activities in which I would indulge to my wanton heart's desire. And I knew what I would do FIRST if there were no God. Wanting to be polite and let other classmates have a chance to speak first, I was silent.

And so was the rest of the class. The professor apparently mistook our silence for class concession that if God excused Himself from our world, we would continue business as usual. He proceeded to verbalize his agreement and added his thoughts.

"No," he said, "I don't think I would lead my life any differently, either. I would be faithful to my wife and treat people as I do now." He concluded, "My life would be about the same." He started into his next subject of absurdity. Completely taken aback at his conclusion, I interrupted him.

"I must say, that if there was no God, I know my life would be radically different."

"Oh really, Angela? Well, why don't you tell how your life would be different, given there was no God."

"I am *quite* sure I would be promiscuous." He looked

surprised, and so did the class, and so did I.

"Ahem...well...well...thank you for your honesty. You have probably been the only truthful one among us."

That was only the *beginning* of what I could have said had I not shown some restraint. I walked out of the class in amazement. Why was it so hard for these folks to admit that their lives would be complete wrecks without the grace of God? The lecture provoked a desire in me to examine my own life.

> *"Search me, O God, and know my heart;*
> *Try me, and know my anxieties;*
> *And see if there is any wicked way in me,*
> *And lead me in the way everlasting."*
> *Psalm 139:23–24*

"Any wicked way" includes lust, religious pride, gluttony, gossip, laziness, judgment, anger, envy, etc. *Anything* that is contrary to the pure, lovely, and holy nature of God. So why do we deny the evil that hides within our hearts? Why are we pure in our own eyes but yet not washed from our filthiness? I'm not sure why we want to cover it up. But the good news is that God has come to set every one of us free from the captivity of our own deceit. He is gracious in His forgiveness.

And now everyone knows what lurks foremost in my heart. Including my mother. Oh dear. But I think she has known all along!

My Zinnia Friend

"My servants shall sing for joy of heart."
Isaiah 65:14

About three and a half minutes into the talk I was giving, I was tempted to say, "And in conclusion, my last point is…" My journal entry that night reflects how I was feeling. *"Speaking to the group of women tonight reminded me of what it must be like to wade through a thick and muddy swamp wearing heavy boots: Exhausting."*

One of my greatest joys is to share with women. Most females can instantly relate, jumping into one another's hearts and lives. Regardless of ages and backgrounds, we share a common thread that weaves us so beautifully together. I smile as I remember such times. They have been life-giving, filled with warmth and pleasure. As evidenced by the above journal entry, other gatherings have been just as memorable, though the memories are of a slightly different nature.

*None are so old
as those who have outlived enthusiasm.*

—Henry David Thoreau

Just for the record, I am not so ego-starved that I presume everyone needs to embrace and be excited about *me* and *my* thoughts. But truthfully, I don't think these women would have been any more stimulated if Mother Teresa, Mary Poppins, or Joan of Arc was in their midst.

As I continued speaking on that rather challenging night, I

was so grateful to see the ending points of my outline. Despite the difficulty of the presentation, I had another reason to be thankful. I saw a very special face in the crowd sitting near the front of the auditorium. Her eyes were full of life and her face was radiant as she smiled at me. She reminded me of a red zinnia peering out above a field of flowers that were withered and dry. A few other blossoms were scattered within the crowd that I enjoyed looking upon, but the zinnia was especially catching to my eye.

Fresh. Lovely. Fragrant. A happy flower.

After the session was over, I had the opportunity to be introduced to the zinnia. Her name was Lenore and she was celebrating seventy-nine years of living. She was a delightful combination of exuberance, warmth, and kindness. Writing in my journal that night, I thought of Lenore. I was reminded of something I have observed my mother do in her years of gardening. Invariably, she will walk past a pot of my geraniums, zinnias, or petunias, and pinch back the dead and fading blossoms. This step is called "dead-heading." In doing this, you provide opportunity for the new growth to burst forth in color and multiplication of new blossoms. I am not suggesting that any of these women needed to be dead-headed. But after an evening with some of them, I will readily admit I was prompted to pray, "Lord, if I ever needed to be dead-headed, would you please just give me a nice pinch?"

Jesus speaks of the process of pruning in John 15:2: "I am the Real Vine and my Father is the Farmer. He cuts off every branch of me that doesn't bear grapes. And every branch that is grape-bearing he prunes back so it will bear even more" (*The Message*). The spiritual application of dead-heading or pruning may be painful in our lives. It is necessary, though, so our lives may be prolific in new growth. I am sure Lenore had welcomed the process of the Lord's pruning in her many years. One of the many fruits of the Spirit borne so abundantly in her life was joy.

We are to be the fragrance of the Lord to those who are perishing. If I had not been a Christian, I know I would have been drawn to the life-giving fragrance that was in Lenore. To the joy bubbling in her heart and spilling over to her face! But I can't truthfully say that about some Christians whom I have known. I have met a lot of *old* women. Perhaps not so much in age as in their attitude—dried and withered. They have outlived their enthusiasm. Your age is not the issue. Have you allowed the Lord to prune and dead-head the fading blossoms? He has designed us this way for a purpose: that His joy might be ours so that we might make it known to others.

If you have been acting rather sour and withered about life—you know, a dead-head—ask the Lord to give you a good pinch! It will make you feel better when those new petals of joy and life come springing up. You, too, can be a zinnia!

The Upside-Down Night

"Be glad in the Lord and rejoice,
you righteous; and shout for joy,
all you upright in heart!"
Psalm 32:11

Of all the many types of men that I think are wonderful, Jewish men have always particularly caught my attention. An appropriate magnet graces my refrigerator even as I write: *World's Best Jewish Lover*. As if I would know. It is strategically placed over my *Pledge to Abstinence* card that I filled out a couple of decades ago. I will leave them both up until it is fit to remove one of them—hopefully the second! My love for Israel has inevitably contributed to my particular fondness for Jewish men.

Such was the case my first couple of years as a nurse. The dark-eyed medical student who treated the nurses and patients with genuine kindness made an indelible impression on me. He was compassionate, empathetic, intelligent, and very handsome. When I learned that he was Jewish, I was even more intrigued. Okay, smitten. Anytime he walked onto the unit, I went into cardiac spasms. He was always quick to flash me one of those blinding smiles, but unfortunately we never had a conversation. Until the eventful night.

It was an extremely frantic midnight shift. There was no temptation to get sleepy because of the challenge of very sick patients who required a great deal of care. My most trying patient was Odie Englebert. That was his name. Fifteen years later, I remember it as clearly as that night. The reason I can never forget dear Odie is because while he was a patient on our unit, he would use his call light as one of his aerobic activities—the great thumb punch. It was not uncommon to get twenty or more calls in eight hours. This would not have been a problem if he had been my only patient.

Despite his love for the call bell, however, I grew very fond of Odie. We had wonderful conversations during those times when he could not sleep and I was not so busy.

On this particularly overwhelming night, he was having his thumb workout. Nothing life-threatening.

"Will you straighten my sheets?"

"It is hot in here."

"Now it is cold."

"Please bring me some water."

"I need orange juice."

"Another blanket, please."

These requests were made at about fifteen minute intervals. Perhaps I needed a waitress short order pad instead of my nursing clipboard. It was time for some boundaries.

"Listen Odie, I need you to think of *every single potential maybe or possible wannas* that you might need, because I absolutely cannot keep coming in here every fifteen minutes. Is there anything you need scratched, moved, adjusted, or brought to you?"

"No," he pleasantly replied. "I can't think of a thing."

"Are you sure?"

"No, I'm fine, Angela. Thank you."

"Okay Odie," I replied a bit warily. "Sleep well." Closing the door for three seconds, I opened it and stuck my head in. "Are you *sure* I can't get anything for you?"

"No."

Satisfied that he would go to sleep, I raced back to the nursing station and started my nursing documentation, which was several hours behind schedule. Now I have deliberately withheld information about Odie: he was paralyzed except for minimal use of his upper extremities.

You are most likely thinking..."Well, you wretched excuse for a human being. Why were you not oozing compassionate care upon this poor man?" This thought crossed my mind on occasion. And I couldn't agree more. I did leak compassion at times, and at others I wanted to yank his call bell out of the wall and dismantle it. This was one of *those* nights. After no less than five minutes of illegibly scrawling on the charts, I saw the call light come on. With that obnoxious grating buzz. Not once but incessantly. Throwing my pen across the room in frustration, I bounded down the hall toward room 384. Pushing the door open I started in on dear Odie before I was across the threshold.

"Odie Englebert!!! I *need* you to cooperate..." My voice trailed off. Standing in the room, talking with the other patient, was the Jewish resident and an attending physician. And both were looking at me as if to say, "This nurse appears upset—distraught—all because of this dear helpless patient." Odie was just smiling at me innocently.

I was horrified. Simply horrified.

Thankful that it was semi-dark, I gulped. My face was warm with color. Suddenly I had the sweetness of a true saint come down in the flesh. In a gentle voice oozing with compassion, tenderness, and subtle hypocrisy I said, "Yes Odie, did you need something, sweetie?"

While speaking to him, I leaned over with my most ethereal look.

"Will you make sure my call light is working?"

Silently I screamed, "Aaagggggghhhhh!" If I had said what I was thinking and did what I was tempted to do, it would have contorted the ethereal look I was working so hard to maintain. "Yes Odie, it is working fine. Is there anything else I can get for you? Some juice, ice chips, something for pain?" (An overdose?)

"No."

Gliding toward the door, I was thrilled to see the two doctors following me. They began asking questions about the other patient, who shared Odie's room, and I was answering them with a professional astuteness that I felt sure would impress them. During my dialogue with them, I noticed that the resident kept looking at my name tag. He seemed to be studying it intently. He looked back up at me and smiled.

"He's looking at my name tag!" I thought to myself. "He wants to know my name!" Thrilled beyond words could not describe how I felt—absolutely and utterly and *completely* overjoyed.

We finished our medical conversation and they graciously thanked me for my help and said good-bye. There have been few men in my life who have been able to produce that glow-in-the-dark kind of feeling. This was one of them. Suddenly, I was filled with dread that I had lipstick on my teeth while talking and smiling to this enchanting creature/medical student. Floating to the bathroom, I sang softly to myself.

"He wanted to know my name...he wanted to know my name..."

Dreamily, I smiled into the mirror and was thrilled to see there was no lipstick. I was also relieved to see that my hair was *looking good!* Turning away, I happened to glance at my name tag.

It was upside down. The blasted thing was upside down. No

wonder he was looking at it so interestedly. Most likely he was thinking, *Not only was she frustrated with poor Odie, she is ditzy.*

Scriptures remind us frequently to desire hearts without deceit, to be upright and pure in heart without false motives. Mine had clearly been revealed to me. Years later I am enjoying a dear friendship with that Jewish doctor and especially his wife. Fortunately, I am over the cardiac problem that I had when near him!

I desire that my heart will be upright at all times and that I am not tempted to pretend to be who I am not. For we can't fake a pure heart for very long. When dear Odie died, I attended his funeral with sadness, but also gratefulness and laughter as I thought of the ways God had used him to reveal some things in my life. When your "Odies" come along—remember Who is watching!

Picture Perfect

"Charm can mislead and beauty soon fades.
The woman to be admired and praised
is the woman who lives in the fear of God."
Proverbs 31:30, The Message

As I looked at the woman in the photographs, I agreed with my friend. "She really is beautiful." Her luminous eyes were large and captivating. The flawless and refined complexion was to be admired. Full and defined lips smiled with a hint of allure. Wisps of hair surrounded her face, as if coyly flirting with her exquisite features. Mystique and charm emanated from her.

"Yes," I consented again, "she is quite stunning. However, she doesn't look a *thing* like me!"

We both burst out laughing. My friend was having his pictures made for a photo shoot and asked me to come along. For the fun of it, I let the photographer take some shots of me. A cosmetic artist (truly, she was that!) prepared my hair and makeup. Although I thought they were lovely pictures, there was no point in purchasing photographs of a woman whom I hardly recognized! Even my optimistic imagination could not be persuaded to believe she was really me. The only things that looked familiar were the clothes I was wearing.

So often we are quick to say, "That is a great picture of you" or "What a terrible picture of me." In a group photograph, we usually look at our own faces first. Everyone else can look homely for all you care, as long as that cute little face of yours is picture perfect. Now if you are not guilty of vanity as most females are, then you are excused from this theory. I will admit that this vanity is true of me, only it is usually not my face I look for initially, but whether the camera angle was flattering to my hips.

You probably think this is a lead-in on the sinfulness of vanity. Or that I will discourse from Proverbs about the deceitfulness of charm and beauty. It wouldn't even cross my mind because I believe the Lord *wants* us to be beautiful women. He is applauding our beauty! And I am not just talking about inward beauty, but beauty on the outside as well! This is not about being sexy or seductive, but *attractive. Lovely. Beautiful.* And this attractiveness comes in an infinite number of definitions. Nicole Johnson talks of beauty in her book, *Fresh-Brewed Life.* "Beauty is embraced because we don't have it all together, and we are trusting God in a more radical way than ever before to make something beautiful out of our surrendered lives." The surrender...ahhh, that is what He wants. And most of all I need to surrender my attitude.

When we honor the value and beauty of our bodies, we are honoring the Creator who formed us. I'm not talking about looking fabulous for a professional photographer. Those pictures are often just a shell of who we really are; the flaws have been diminished and the positives enhanced. What are we when the normal lights come on? Okay, in all honesty...*embarrassed!* Sometimes I am shocked when I see all of the imperfections. Some can be changed but most of them are here to stay. If I allow my focus to be on them, they become even bigger than they really are.

As wild as my imagination is, I am challenged in believing that a wonderful man could love me unconditionally physically. My roommate looked at me in complete amazement many years ago when I told her I was comfortable with the idea of marrying someone who was blind. She thought I was trying to be funny. I was not. At times like that, reflect upon the words of Psalm 139:14: "I am fearfully and wonderfully made; marvelous are Your works, and that my soul knows very well." Let's just hope the man knows it.

Do I believe that God made mistakes in the specifics of how He made me?

Sometimes.

So Lord, let my heart and mind embrace the truth of Your word. Only when I allow myself to feed upon the inescapable advertisements and their parameters of beauty do I feel intimidated and inferior. It's the comparison monster. As you can tell, I haven't reached the end of the journey nor have I cut off the head of the dragon triumphantly. But I have made a few dents!

For me, it's all about *choosing* to accept that God has a special and unique design for my life. God did not make a mistake, as simplistic and elementary as that sounds. And on those days when I am feeling especially daunted by the multitudes of lovely women…hot pink toenail polish does wonders.

Christmas Mourning

"God resists the proud,
but gives grace to the humble."
James 4:6

The sounds of little sobs filled the air. Christmas Day is a dreadful time to be sad. It is an even worse day to have to attend a funeral. Especially when the untimely death of the beloved was your fault. That would be me I am speaking of, and I write with utmost regret and remorse.

Tears ran freely down my cheeks as I watched my young nieces Caroline and Lydia throw flowers onto the freshly turned mound of dirt. The silk blooms were marked-down, inexpensive blossoms, but these little girls laid them as reverently as if they were exquisite hybrid bouquets. We adults had not taken the time nor interest in bonding with Ebenezer, the dearly departed kitten. Together we sang a woeful song and my brother-in-law, Shane, prayed a most appropriate prayer for a freshly demised feline. Together we walked silently and soberly into the house. All that was lacking was a funeral dirge to make the scene complete. When I saw my sister Shawn shaking silently in laughter, I was compelled to kick her in the ankle. There is always an insensitive, cold-hearted one in the crowd.

Caroline had especially loved the two new additions my mother had gotten to help chase the squirrels ("chase" sounds nicer than kill, destroy, and maim) that were demolishing her flowers and garden. She and Lydia were given the privilege of naming them. The stately titles of Ebenezer and Marley were bestowed upon the scraggly barn cats. Both nieces instantly loved them with the abandonment that only six- and three-year-old hearts can have for furry felines. "Survivor and Miracle" would have been more appropriate names after being loved so capriciously by my nieces. The two kittens seemed to adapt to the nurturing squeezes and ungainly positioning, as evidenced by their incessant purrs. But now poor Ebenezer had truly met the Ghost of Christmas, thanks to me.

Just a few minutes before the tragedy, I had been outside with the girls admiring our newborn basset puppies. Molly had given birth to four little ones on Christmas Eve, and was quite the doting mother. Oskar, on the other hand, was more interested in being scratched on his belly than he was in protecting the four puppies he had sired. As we were leaving the pen, he barked frantically to come with us. Molly wanted to follow as well. It seemed like a nice idea. "Let's let the dogs out for a walk, girls." What I didn't know is that Molly had her hormonally disturbed heart set on eating more than our leftovers for her Christmas dinner. Women can do the strangest things when their hormones are out of kilter.

"But Sissy..." Caroline's voiced dragged in hesitation, "I don't think we should." Pointing to the two balls of fur she had clasped to her chest. "What about Ebenezer and Marley?"

"Oh Caroline, don't you worry. Oskar and Molly won't hurt those kittens." Her little face looked uncertain. She tried again, "Well Sissy, I don't think we should..."

"Trust me, Caroline. Everything will be *fine*." She still did not look convinced. Lydia shook her head in support of Caroline, while sucking on her two fingers.

Letting the dogs out, I went into the garage to look at something. From a distance I heard barking and yeowing, along with the terrified shrill screams of my sweet little nieces. Caroline tried bravely to rescue her beloved Ebenezer from none other than the jaws of death, which happened to be in the mouth of a very hormonal mother dog.

"SISSY! SISSSSYYY!!!!!" Racing across the yard, I took the limp and bedraggled Ebenezer from her hands. Sobbing uncontrollably, she looked up at me. "Why didn't you come, Sissy, why didn't you come?"

The eyes of my eyes are opened.

—*e. e. cummings*

Because I am an arrogant so-and-so I thought, too full of pride to listen to the wisdom of a six-year-old. Lydia was crying because Caroline was crying, and now I have tears as I remember. No, I'm not grieving about Ebenezer. That took about sixty seconds. I'm still in shame of what happened. Caroline was so insistent on not taking out the dogs, she was beginning to irritate me. Then I was determined not to give in to her, all because of my stubbornness and pride. I learned a lesson that Christmas morning through such simple instruments. A child. A kitten.

Christmas mourning transformed into Christmas grace.

Humiliation changed to humility. Grace to the humble.

Pink Throw Up

*"I am exceedingly joyful
in all our tribulation."*
2 Corinthians 7:4b

My six-year-old niece, Caroline, and I were shopping together one spring morning. We were walking hand in hand when she suddenly announced, "Sissy, I am going to be sick." And with that she opened her mouth and threw up. I held my arms around her until her mission was completed. Understandably, she was embarrassed and began crying.

"Look Caroline!" I said, pointing to the sidewalk. "It's pink!" Enthusiastically, I proclaimed, "Now *that* is the prettiest throw up I have *ever* seen! Amazing!" She looked up at me incredulously and so did everyone else passing us.

Pointing to her morning breakfast of fresh strawberries and cream, which was now splattered on the sidewalk, my voice filled with wonder. I said, "You know, most people have nasty, ugly, gross throw up, but yours is bee-U-tiful!"

She grinned weakly at me and seemed to be feeling better already.

Although our circumstances can sometimes be out of our control, it is our attitude that affects how we respond to them. Louis Pasteur once said, "The Greeks have given us one of the most beautiful words of our language, the word enthusiasm— a god within." Pasteur continued, "The grandeur of the acts of men is measured by the inspiration from which they spring. Happy is he who bears God within."

How enthusiastic are you about living? I'm not suggesting that we strive for those "Ha Ha" moments every second of every day. Life is sometimes a challenge not only from day to day, but sometimes second to second. Our circumstances are not always tidy nor do the *surprises* always fit in a planner. But if "God truly is within," as Pasteur suggested, then how can we not be enthusiastic about life? Actually, it was the Bible that made that declaration before Pasteur did. "In Him we live and move and have our being" (Acts 17:28*a*). "He who is in you is greater than he who is in the world" (1 John 4:4*b*).

Life is challenging at times. However, our attitude affects how we respond to the kids throwing up in public places, the jeans that are suddenly too tight, the uncooperative husband, or, in my case, the missing husband.

What of life when it is smooth for a season? For instance, the children are docile and angelic, your husband is romantic and sensitive, there is sufficient money in the checking account, and your jeans are loose. Is your heart attitude one of grate- fulness? The English priest and poet George Herbert expressed this need: "Thou that hast given so much to me, give one thing more—a grateful heart." When my heart attitude is one of gratefulness for the many gifts that have been given to me, it is amazing how my attitude changes toward the negative things.

The morning that Caroline up-chucked her strawberries, I was so thrilled to have her visiting me that I didn't care that it splattered all over my brand new khaki pants that were NOT on sale! Nor did I care that I had to clean it up out of courtesy to the merchants. But there have been those moments when I did not enjoy those throw-up kind of days and events. And my attitude has not been so pleasant. Ahhhh, but on those occa- sions when I have responded with optimism and a positive out- look, the atmosphere of the challenging events was much less daunting and more easily managed.

Our responses to life's negative events so easily spill over into the lives of others. Reactions can be pessimistic or positive, making those involved either miserable or grateful to have you around. We can't avoid the reality that circumstances of life can simply be messy. The unexpected mayhem of the day. Being stuck in traffic for hours. Plans and goals totally and completely amuck. Those unavoidable kinks in the schedule. The cake that falls. A toilet that overflows while the cake is falling. Both on the day of your dinner party. It happens. Those are the times when you can pray an old Hasidic prayer, "I know the Lord will help—but help me Lord until You help."

On the nights when you fall into bed ever so grateful that you survived, I hope you'll have a soft whimsical smile upon your lips as you recount the events of the day. Yes, there were moments of panic, but you kept moving with the underlying energy of His joy that was smack in the middle of the unexpected chaos. I hope that your outlook on life will be as insightful as the beloved character of Winnie the Pooh, who wisely said, "Every day is full of wonderful!"

A Whole Lot Of
Changing Going On

*"Now may the God of peace Himself
sanctify you completely;
and may your whole spirit, soul,
and body be preserved blameless at the coming
of our Lord Jesus Christ."*
1 Thessalonians 5:23

Having survived the emotional hurdle of turning forty without being driven to drugs, alcohol, or promiscuity, I was somewhat relieved. And that is when I really appreciated the promise of 1 Thessalonians that my body would be preserved. A newborn experiences an array of physical changes. Their umbilical cord falls off, their head shapes up, skin tones even out, and they start growing hair. They get prettier. Oh, I had some changes coming up, but they were not headed in the direction of pretty. Denial shields you only for a short season. "You shall know the truth and the truth will set you free," says the Good Book. In this case, the truth made me depressed.

Shortly after my crossover into the abyss, I was washing my hair in the shower. Trying my new conditioner for the first time, I was attempting to read the directions so as to learn how long it should stay in my hair. This was a product that was made in Germany and sold in the US. To my irritation, I discovered it was written in German. "Now, how in the world am I supposed to know how long it should stay on," I muttered to myself, completely annoyed. To my surprise, dismay, and overwhelming horror, I discovered that when I held the container *further* away from my eyes, I could read the directions ever so clearly...in English. *Oh dear.*

About this time, I also noticed that wisdom was sprouting from my hair. Not just a few sprouts but a whole head full. Not wanting to step across the line of dyeing my hair, I started using a shampoo rinse. I did *not* need to start dyeing my hair. Nothing so drastic or permanent or anything like that. Mine was just a simple rinse. *Blatant denial.* My moment of revelation came one day when I was out in my mother's yard picking flowers for an arrangement. I was enjoying a pleasant afternoon mist while cutting the different greeneries. On the way back to my home, I noticed one of my favorite stores having its annual fall sale. This store is a bit pricey, but you can get great bargains twice a year. I usually try to look somewhat together and presentable when I shop there, but today was an exception. Finding a great sweater for a fraction of the price, I made my way to the counter. The sales clerk looked at me rather quizzically. Leaning over, she whispered in my ear, "Do you dye your hair?" Looking at her as if she had asked me for a kiss, I recoiled in horror.

"*Me*," I squeaked, "dye my hair?! Why ever would you ask?" My mind was rationalizing, "No, Angela, you do not dye your hair. You really don't. It's a rinse. Not even in the same category."

She whispered again, "Well, you have black driblets running down your face." Bursting into laughter, I picked up my package and made my way out the door, careful not to drip on the clothes.

It was just a few weeks later when I woke up one morning and couldn't move. Not to the right or left or up or down. My back was completely rigid. I couldn't even roll over. There was no phone by my bed so I thought I might just die peacefully.

Muttering that this is why everyone should be married, just in case they need a good push out of bed, I managed to maneuver myself with my hands before landing with an ungraceful splat on my knees. There I stayed and cried for about an hour. It was quite pitiful and moving, I assure you. The short version of a long story is that a good friend rescued me and dropped me off at my physician's office. He enthusiastically told me that these sorts of things sometimes happen as we get older. Well, as far am I am concerned, it is essential that I get married just in case I need some help getting out of bed again. Until then, a portable phone would be a good idea.

When grace is joined with wrinkles,
it is adorable.
There is an unspeakable dawn
in happy old age.

—*Victor Hugo*

Michelangelo once prayed, "Lord let me see the glory in every place." And perhaps that is why he enjoyed painting so many older women! There really is a certain kind of glory in getting older. All of my life I have appreciated the exhortation for the older women to teach the younger. And I have availed myself of many godly women who had experienced so much more of life than I had. They were able to share from wisdom and experiences gained through the years. And now I think I am fast approaching that older category. I've even had a couple of girls ask for advice for their *honeymoon night*, which nearly pushed me over the edge. Somehow I don't think making up an answer that sounds wise is an option, although it worked for the moment!

Someone has said, "You only live once—but if you work it right, once is enough." That sage piece of advice is enough to remind me that I don't have even a single moment to waste lamenting over getting older...a *sure* sign of old age.

The Signature
Of His Hand

"For we are His workmanship,
created in Christ Jesus for good works,
which God prepared beforehand
that we should walk in them. "
Ephesians 2:10

Crossing the chasm from "thirty-something" to forty could only be compared to a birth experience. Especially the labor part. Just like one of those many infants I have seen who come kicking and screaming into the world, I too felt the compression of forceps wrapped around my head. They were harsh and unyielding, firmly pulling me into cold and sterile surroundings.

The Unknown. Terrifying. Formidable.

Thus began my journey. *Twisting and writhing,* as if my one hundred and "umm humm" pounds of resistance would allow me to go in the opposite direction, I fought the good fight. Denial was no longer working and reality was excruciating. If I could have stayed in the safe and warm environment of the "thirty-somethings," I would have. I have observed so many little ones scoot backwards into the birth canal until another big contraction propels them up front. That would be me, a big forty-year-old baby. I even had the sensation of a cone-shaped head, a wet bottom, and a dimpled rear end when it was all over.

After I was actually delivered into what I thought was the abyss of forty, I was just so grateful to have survived that I was unusually silent for a few days. And then I adjusted my attitude and decided to continue to enjoy life as usual. After all, other than contributing to my demise, there were not a lot of choices. If you think I am being dramatic about this life change, I could not agree more. And every dismal thought was darker than the ink which you read. Without even a smidge of exaggeration.

Fortunately for me, during that transitional time I read a word study on the word *workmanship*. In the Greek it is translated as *poiema*, from which the verb *poieo* is derived, which means "to make." Poetry and poem are derivatives of *poieo*. It will sound like more than Greek to you in just a moment. For *poieo* is a word that signifies a design produced by an artisan. *Poiema* emphasizes God as the Master Designer, the universe being His creation and the redeemed believer as His new creation. We are God's poem, His work of art.

Whatever age I am or become, it is encouraging for me to think of my life as an ongoing poem. He is adding verses each day, line upon line, precept upon precept. His workmanship is continually being created upon the passing of every day. And as I reach each new milestone of years, I am grateful in understanding that He will continue to paint the colors of His grace upon my life.

His creation of me, by a skilled artisan, my Designer. His words are a chronicle and testament of Divine Workmanship. My poem—a work of art—my life, worthy of a great price, because of the signature of the Artist.

No Trespassing

"Love one another with brotherly affection
[as members of one family],
giving precedence and showing honor
to one another."
Romans 12:10, Amplified

While out walking one evening in my neighborhood, I paused at a picket fence surrounding the backyard of a nearby home. Although I had driven or walked past the yard countless times, I had *looked* but never *seen* it as I did that night. The picket fence was an aesthetic addition to this home. However, it also served a purpose—keeping intruders out in a pleasant, cordial sort of way. The fence contained within its borders things that were precious to this family, such as children and pets, an herb garden, and carefully tended flower beds.

The following days, I observed the yard surrounded by the fence a little more carefully. My time of reflection was much more than the studying of architecture. It's as if there was an imaginary welcome sign over the arched door that said, "Angela, you are invited to pause, see, and listen."

What I have been learning since that night is a principle in relationships that has been invaluable—the importance of emotional boundaries. I'm not speaking of a fortress that is intimidating and impenetrable, but rather a means of protecting the treasures of one's life.

The impression of a picket fence is one that appeals to me. Through it, one can catch glimpses of the beauty beyond. It is inviting and pleasant. However, this particular door that enters into the garden is made to be opened from the inside. Thus, you must be invited to come in.

For a number of years, I have been very open about issues of my heart and life, sometimes revealing things that were very precious to me. And at times I have allowed people into my backyard, so to speak, who did not always love or cherish the things that were planted there. Some have watered the young and tender life that was growing. Others have appreciated the more maturing plants while encouraging the painful pruning process that results in more prolific growth. Some, with kindness and compassion, have pointed to weeds that I did not see. If I needed their assistance, they have helped me pull and tend to the unwanted growth.

There have been some visitors in my garden who have not walked as carefully as others. They have stomped on some of the germinating plants, from carelessness or because they could not appreciate their unique beauty. Perhaps they have even tried to wrench them from the earth because they thought they did not belong in my garden. They did not regard them as meaningful to me. Some have even been so bold as to attempt to transplant cuttings from their garden that they thought I needed. Their lack of respect for these tender plants has often caused bruising in the process.

Each of us has places in our heart and emotions that are sacred. These hallowed places are not to be exposed and opened to just anyone. They are to be guarded and protected for the treasure and value that lies therein. The picket fence was a gentle reminder that I am the keeper of my garden, and I am to tend it carefully.

The elements of nature are sometimes destructive to a natural garden. A wise gardener will do all that is possible to protect the plants, especially the young and vulnerable ones.

Elements in the *human* nature can wreak havoc on the garden of our hearts. I'm speaking of the dreams and ideas that God has scattered within the dark and quiet places of our hearts.

Detrimental forces come in various shapes and sizes ...friends and family. People that you love. Just as the very elements of nature can be destructive, so can the individuals who attempt to wrench away your dreams. They trample cherished hopes and longings, even with good intentions. In this process they will damage the very root system, thus causing dreams to wilt and ultimately die.

What is our responsibility in tending our garden? It takes courage to say "no" to everyone who wants to tromp into your yard without regard or respect for the unique beauty that lies therein. If you are like me, and have at times been too inviting and welcoming to the voices and opinions of the countless "well-meaning ones," the transition can be unfamiliar and uncomfortable for you and your visitors. Some are accustomed to waltzing freely into your yard, regardless of an invitation. Initially, they might bump their noses up against the fence, thus rattling it and demanding to come in. But as you learn to keep them at a proper distance, you will find that it becomes more familiar and comfortable terrain. You can smile at them from behind your fence and even lean over it while having a pleasant conversation. But you are ever mindful that you have a cordial but firm barrier between you and the destructive elements of personality and opinions. You are not required to invite them in and would be wise not to do so.

I am completely astounded at the questions that people will ask me that could very appropriately be answered, "It is none of your business." At times I have wanted to be *just* as inappropriate and ask, "How many times a week do you have sex?" Fortunately, His grace has restored me.

The following prayer is one that I read at a time when I had experienced the pain and confusion that comes from listening to too many voices. I pray this as a reminder to follow God's voice first and above all others.

> *To listen to what it is that makes my heart glad*
> *and to follow where it leads.*
> *May joy, not guilt,*
> *Your voice and not the voice of others,*
> *Your will, not my willfulness,*
> *be the guides that lead me to my vocation.*
> *Help me to unearth the passions of my heart*
> *that lay buried in my youth.*
> *And help me to go over that ground again and again*
> *until I can hold in my hands,*
> *hold and treasure,*
> *Your calling on my life.*
> *—Ken Gire, in his book* Windows of the Soul

Yes, Father.
Amen.

Elastic and Plastic

"The King's daughter is all glorious within."
Psalm 45:13, NASB

Lydia watched me intently and silently while sucking on her three fingers. My three-year-old niece was deeply engrossed in my activity, studying my every move. Only intense curiosity would cause her to remove her fingers long enough to ask her question.

"Whatcha doin, Sissy? Why you puttin all dat cream on yoh face?"

"Because your Sissy is vain, darling."

"Oh." Pausing, she added with enthusiasm, "Me too! Put some cream on my face, Sissy!"

As I was rubbing the age-defying cream on her porcelain skin, I thought of Queen Esther. I was reminded of the year of beauty rituals she undertook before being presented to King Xerxes. This makes me feel better about slathering lotion on my face. I'm not ashamed to say I would drink it by the bottle if it would help ward off the evil spirits of wrinkles. What did Esther do besides soak in mud packs and olive oil for a year? If plastic surgery had been an option, would she have pursued it?

This thought was prompted by a nursing seminar that I had recently attended, a plastic surgery update. After the eight-hour session was over, I had seen no less than four hundred slides of women in the most imaginative shapes and sizes.

There were bottoms that had been artistically contoured. Stomachs that were tucked. Breasts enlarged. Faces stretched and lifted. Sagging arms made firm. Skinny calves enhanced and made curvaceous. And noses skillfully recreated.

Oh, and don't forget the lips. Now with just a few injections of bovine collagen, you, too, can have full pouty lips. It used to be that only the rich and famous had plastic surgery. Now anyone with a wrinkle or two and a credit card with an exorbitant limit qualifies.

That afternoon I was telling my neighbor that I left the seminar rather subdued. My rear end was dragging, so to speak. Fortunately, there is a procedure that can take care of a droopy bottom as well. My question after this enlightening update was, "Can we not just be a little flawed and accept our ages gracefully?"

It's fairly obvious that our society is saturated with this quest for eternal beauty and youth. This trend seems to have accelerated in recent years. The timing is somewhat unfortunate for me…*just* as I am getting in that *older age bracket!* The desire to produce that drop-dead gorgeous look is, sadly enough, sometimes yielding just that; death statistics are rising alarmingly from invasive cosmetic procedures.

In a medical unit that I worked in, one of our doctors was learning how to perform liposuction. In order to be certified in this procedure, he was accumulating his required hours from volunteers within the nursing staff—those who were interested, that is. Several of the nurses were enthusiastically signing up. I knew the only thing I really needed to sign was the register log at the gym. Someone asked if I was going to participate in the event.

"No. Although I appreciate the opportunity, I would really like to have my rear end enlarged and would hereby solicit all your leftovers."

I'll admit, I found the whole event a bit amusing. This particular doctor was one whom I enjoyed working with. He came in one morning to do a circumcision on one of the newborns.

As I was strapping in the little guy, I asked, "Would you like a scalpel or a vacuum?" He gave me a look as if to say, "I would *really* like to liposuction your tongue."

If one is a greyhound, why try to look like a Pekingese?

—Dame Edith Sitwell

If you are like me and don't want the invasive routes for a sleek and smooth body, even if it is free, there is a wonderful alternative. There is now an abundance of creams advertised with promises of reducing your thighs and firming your breasts *and* removing cellulite and spider veins. The seaweed wrap is for the larger-than-life areas and will take off a couple of inches. Simply wrap sheets of seaweed around your thighs, cover the area in plastic wrap and heat it with a blow dryer. If you drink water, I suspect that all of your fat cells blow up. So if you don't mind a little dehydration and potential electrolyte imbalance, "Voila! Hello to sleek, svelte thighs!"

The one that really caught my attention was "Decolletage." Within two hours of rubbing this miraculous cream on your breasts, they are guaranteed to increase two sizes. Incredible! I didn't know if this resulted from extra-cellular fluid being drained from brain cells into breast tissue or from some other reservoir of fluid. I wouldn't mind rerouting some from my derriere. As evidenced by the fact that I have not yet changed bra sizes, I can't produce any raving reports.

Obviously, I have spent a great deal of time thinking about this issue of the perfect body. What is the balance? Yes, healthy habits are important, such as exercise and nutritional wisdom. But what do we do about the inevitable effects of aging? Paper sacks could be nice.

Changing my attitude toward myself has been a step forward for me. No, I am not perfect, nor will I ever be perfect. Yes, I continue to work on the discipline of exercising and eating right. And I use creams and masks and all the rest of the messy goos. But what about my heart attitude toward myself? Take off the positives of my exterior and who am I? Add a few more flaws and who am I then?

The psalmist writes: "The King's daughter is all glorious within" (Psalm 45:13 NASB) This is conflicting with the countless advertisements that flaunt the message that unless we are beautiful and flawless on the outside, we are lacking. At a deficit. At times I have to adamantly remind myself that this is not my goal. Now I am not at all discounting that realistic and healthy weight is something to be desired. But it is our attitude that weighs most of all. Too often I am intimidated by beautiful women. Being around them produces a longing to be perfect, and I am reminded of my flaws. I am not ashamed to say that because I am reminded to refocus my heart attitude toward the desire for true and lasting beauty.

We can't fake that kind of attitude. It is the recognition that the beauty from within can radiate to our countenance and enhance our confidence. While driving into North Carolina fairly recently, I saw a large billboard that was so refreshing. It simply said, "Smile, You Are Beautiful!" And it wasn't sponsored by a dental association. Without thinking, I found myself smiling and then noticed that I had tears in my eyes at the simple yet profound truth of that billboard.

Whatever size or shape and whatever the multiple flaws are, we are created in the image of the One who knows what true beauty is all about. I am beautiful. You are beautiful. So take a deep breath and smile, sweetie!

For you are beautiful!

The Long Race

"Let us lay aside every weight,
and the sin which so easily ensnares us,
and let us run with endurance
the race that is set before us."
Hebrews 12:1b

The police car trailed me slowly. Wiping the perspiration from my brow, I turned back long enough to give him an apologetic smile. For a brief moment, I considered asking him for a ride. The finish line of the 5K was in the distance. The voices of my friends called me on to completion. As I approached the red ribbon, I threw back my head and arms like I had seen so many Olympic runners do. The cheers and laughter of my friends who had finished at least thirty minutes before me were scintillating. And their good-hearted jabs took away the sting of my dishonor.

Grabbing a bottle of water, I walked over to the police car and apologized for taking so long to complete the course. He was a kindly old gentleman, and I am sure he appreciated the opportunity to nap as I slowly padded along. He congratulated me on finishing last place.

That was my second 5K to run. The only reason I hadn't come in last place at my first attempt in long distance running was that I had taken a short cut.

There was a time when I used to run several miles a day, anywhere from three to five.

In the last three years I have been walking more than running. Before this race, however, I had lulled myself into thinking that I had a reservoir of strength and endurance from which I could draw. My optimism is sometimes out of the bounds of realism.

The whole event could have been terribly discouraging, except I took it as an opportunity to face the fact that I was out of shape. I had two choices: to continue to think about it or to do something.

The Lord seemed to agree with my thoughts, as evidenced by a conversation I had with a new acquaintance. She mentioned that she was running in a marathon the following weekend. She explained that someone had given her a schedule that eased her slowly into running 26 miles. I jokingly accused her of drug usage or hypnosis, which she denied.

It was about this time when I found a journal entry I had written three years earlier. The Lord has often shared with me words of love and affirmation. And at other times they have been…loving, yes, but with more of an emphasis on discipline. These are the kinds of words that make you swallow with difficulty. "*I want you to lose this weight Angela. It has been like the extra luggage and bags that you tend to carry around. Useless and unnecessary. You are tired and weighed down. It is not difficult or complicated to obey. Push through into this freedom. For this is pleasing to me.*" This was a time when I was struggling to lose ten pounds. Okay…fifteen. I needed to get down to…you know…the real weight on my driver's license.

I couldn't deny that the Lord was getting my attention. With a mixture of excitement and trepidation, I started the running program and am making progress that I find most encouraging. *Without the assistance of drugs or hypnosis.* And my driver's license is once again truthful!

Just recently I was talking with one of my good friends who had been applauding me as I crossed the finish line that fall day at the Covered Bridge Run. She doesn't yet know of my new athletic prowess.

"Hey Ange. Why don't you come over and run in the 5K next weekend? I don't want to be last place, so I would really appreciate you coming!"

"Thanks, Lucy. Would love to, but I am going to be out of town. What about next year?!"

SECTION THREE:

Don't Just Sit There, Take Yourself To the Prom

Challenges for renewing ourselves and becoming more like Christ

Christmas Gift

"Lord, my heart is not haughty,
nor mine eyes lofty"
Psalm 131:1a

Driving along the rural country road, I was enjoying the greenery and natural decorations on barns and large farmhouses. My car was decked out in a wreath, and the fragrance of fresh fir limbs from my back seat was a pleasant reminder of the approaching Christmas Day.

As I slowed down for a hound dog to cross the road, my eyes rested on the house trailer that the pitiful creature was ambling toward. Old cars with missing wheels were parked in front. A washing machine was on the lean-to porch, next to a faded floral couch with a broken armpiece. In the window of the front door there was a plastic Santa smiling kindly, his jolly face surrounded by multi-colored lights that blinked spasmodically, casting a rather garish light upon his ample and rosy cheeks.

In the yard between the two rusty cars was a nativity set. Its life-size figures surrounded the infant Savior. One of the wise men was missing his right hand.

By that time, the hound with her dangling udders had reached her destination. I whizzed past the holy family, muttering aloud, "That is *the* tackiest thing I ever did see."

The voice of the Holy Spirit suddenly interrupted Perry Como's "Silent Night." "Angela, you can be *such* a snob. What gives you the authority to declare what is tacky? Did someone make you the Decorating Queen? The Matriarch of Refined Taste? That little tin trailer represents the home of a family with dreams and feelings just like yours. In their own personal way, they are celebrating this season. And furthermore, they just might think *you* are tacky in your decorations."

Well.

Who could deny my arrogance?

In Job 34:19, Elihu reminds Job that God "is not partial to princes, nor does He regard the rich more than the poor, for they are all the work of His hands."

Are you also guilty of looking down upon someone who does not meet your standards of what is acceptable in taste or style? And furthermore, what does your opinion matter unless you are asked? Our heart attitude is to be one of humility toward one another, regarding each as higher than ourselves—the poor and the rich. We can be proud of the most ridiculous things, though perhaps not in obvious ways.

Good breeding consists in concealing how much we think of ourselves and how little we think of the other person.

—*Mark Twain*

Loftiness has a way of disguising itself. Deep in your heart, do you consider yourself just a cut above because of your education? Your family heritage? The school you went to, the church you attend, the places you have traveled, the grades your children make, the occupation of your spouse? Perhaps you would never say it aloud. That's quite understandable. But in the safety of His love, these thoughts are worth considering. The Lord is ever near to soften your heart and cleanse any arrogance or pride. Aren't we just absurd to make our subtle boasts in any earthly possessions or accomplishments? To boast of *anything* except the Lord?

Jesus was as comfortable with the poor as He was with the wealthy. He saw beyond the exterior into the heart of man. He looks upon us and what does He see? Are we decorated with our tacky medals of pride and gain? Or are we adorned with humility? Do we reverence ourselves, our accomplishments, or our pretty things more than we do Him?

There is only one thing to be revered. Humble Savior. Mighty God.

Oh come let us adore Him.

The Good
Night Story

*"Remember His marvelous works
which He has done, His wonders,
and the judgments of His mouth."*
1 Chronicles 16:12

Closing up my journal and stuffing it under my pillow, I rolled over on the small bed. The soothing clacking of the swiftly moving train soon lulled me to sleep. We were crossing the mountains of northern Russia. The journal tucked away was filled with accounts of significant events in my life that had taken place on this trip. I had relinquished to God areas in which I had struggled, and I knew the peace of surrender. I slept soundly as we crossed the barren terrain, en route to a city where we would be meeting with university students.

The purpose of the trip was a student outreach to Ukrainian universities. I was traveling with a team of American doctors, nurses, and attorneys. We had been keeping long and strenuous hours and were all very tired.

The frantic calls of our team leader abruptly interrupted our sleep. Banging on the door, he announced that we had to be off the train in four minutes. Apparently, we had all overslept. Throwing back my covers, I quickly sat up in bed, forgetting I was in the upper berth. Groaning from the pain of my jolted head, I began throwing on my clothes. My roommate and I fumbled around and bumped into one another in the compact berth. We straggled outside, dragging backpacks and hoping everything was zipped and buttoned.

The train whistle blew its lone warning to clear the tracks. We watched it slowly gather speed and fade into the distance. Unknown to me, the train was carrying my cherished journal with it. Gingerly rubbing the bump on my head, I followed my team to the hotel. Several hours later, I had that dreadful sensation of nausea as I realized that my journal was headed in the direction of the uttermost parts of the earth.

I never travel without my diary.
One should always have something
sensational to read on the train.

—*Oscar Wilde,*

The Importance of Being Earnest

Our Ukrainian team leader assured me he would make an attempt to call the train station, but I knew he thought it was a vain request.

What happened in the course of the next ten hours will always be a reminder of God's love and sovereignty. My friend and roommate, Ann, knelt with me and asked for God's intervention. As we prayed for the return of my journal, I knew He could intervene if He wanted to; however, I yielded that desire to Him. Through a remarkable series of events, our prayer was answered. The sheer joy of writing in my journal that very night is a feeling that I still cherish, even several years later. I walk in the full realization that the Lord orders and directs my steps. Even when I make mistakes, His grace covers me.

When the children of Israel were en route to the Promised Land, the Lord told them to erect memorial stones as a reminder of the things He had done for them. Our journals can hold the recordings of those events that are memorial stones in our lives. If you already keep a journal, you know how valuable it is to you. If you don't, I would strongly encourage you to start one at this very chapter of your life.

For, you see, your life is a book in which God is writing His wonderful truths. Over the years I have had journals with pretty and elaborate covers as well as ones that were plain. But none are plain on the inside, for they are all filled with thoughts that reflect the overwhelming goodness, faithfulness, and love of my Father.

The Nekked Truth

*"The wicked flee when no one pursues,
but the righteous are bold as a lion."*
Proverbs 28:1

One morning after getting off work from the hospital, I spotted a yard sale sign and followed the directions into a very nice neighborhood. As I slowed down to look for a parking place, I happened to glance at a house that had a number of full-length windows. There is nothing so unusual about that, except that standing inside one of the windows was a man. A naked man. It is well known across the South that there are two types of nudity: the "naked" and those folks that are "*nekked*." "Naked" implies a rather stately and regal representation—something like Michelangelo's *David*. "Nekked" is more of a homely sort of image and is best pronounced with a southern twang. This gentleman was *nekked*. Oh my.

As he saw my startled face, he grinned. Not exactly feeling like Miss Congeniality, I glared back at him. At his face, that is. As I was busily scowling and making sure that he saw my disapproval, a thought occurred to me. If he was exposing his *"nekked"* self to me, he was most likely doing the same to other innocent folks such as little blue-haired old ladies who might faint, or even worse, to children. Quickly assessing the situation, I considered my options for alleviating this problem other than crashing through the window with my Honda and obliterating this gentleman from his moral misery. Instead, I pulled out a piece of paper and wrote down the address. Not to be deterred by this interruption, I proceeded to the yard sale. After making a few purchases, I drove to the downtown police department.

After being directed to the Department of Complaints, I proceeded to tell my story to a room full of officers, who by all appearances were more interested in eating their sausage biscuits than they were in listening to me. As I related the details of my morning outing, one of the gentlemen paused in his chewing. From one side of his mouth he asked, "Now, now honey, are you *sure* he was *nekked*?" In other words, "You innocent and hysterical female...you must be imagining things." One of my least favorite things in life besides gaining weight is to be talked to condescendingly. If social restraints require restrictive behavior and toleration, I am willing to comply. But it wouldn't even cross my mind to be forbearing when I have been working all night.

Leaning over the counter so that he could clearly see that my pupils were constricted...slowly, slowly, and ever so deliberately, my words resonated throughout that room and bounced off four concrete walls into the ears of about nine men sitting there chewing.

"I will have you know that I see naked men all the time. What I saw was a *nekked* man in the window, and *you*, sir, better be doing something about it."

Coffee cups were suspended in mid air.

Eighteen eyes were fixed on me.

And it was very, very quiet.

A man who reminded me of Boss Hogg stood slowly to his feet and swallowed. He pulled his pants up over his protruding belly and proceeded to fill out a report. In less than three minutes I was out of there and in my car. As I drove off, I noticed my lab jacket on the seat. I laughed aloud as I realized that because I had stood behind the counter, they could have only seen the turtleneck I was wearing and not my nursing scrub pants. They wouldn't have had any indication that I was a nurse!

"Well," I thought. "At least I got their attention."

What happened from that morning saga was that I was called in to testify against the man. He had two former complaints filed on him, and to press charges, one more complaint was needed, which was mine. I was so thankful that I had gone ahead with the charges despite my irritation. He had exposed himself to children and needed to be stopped.

Sometimes it is easier to walk away from controversial issues than get involved.

The decision to participate may be costly to your time and reputation. Queen Esther went before King Xerxes with a request that may have cost her very life (Esther 4). The result was that many Jews' lives were spared. We can turn away from involving ourselves in situations that might very well stretch us beyond our comfort zones. But for the sake of righteousness, we can be as bold as lions if we remember where our source of strength is from. If He is for us, who can defy our just and righteous cause? Ask the Lord to give guidance to your involvement in community and political affairs, and certainly for those so dear to the heart of God—our children, whether born or unborn. Be a voice for those who cannot speak, as described in Proverbs 31:8.

You never know what situations might be waiting just around the corner, or what *window* of opportunity might need your attention!

Harmony of Heart

"Enter your chambers,
and shut your doors behind you;
hide yourself, as it were, for a little moment."
Isaiah 26:20

Anyone acquainted with me knows that I can carry on a conversation with just about anything or anyone. People. Answering machines. Animals. One of the greatest conversations I ever had was with a cow on a farm in Mentone, Alabama. Even language barriers can be easily hurdled with a little creativity and no inhibitions. The point is, I know how to talk. I'm very comfortable with it. It is something I do very well, although at times I do it too much.

During a class I was taking with poet and author Luci Shaw last summer, she announced that we would be having a day of silence. Our course was entitled "Keeping a Reflective Journal" and was held on an island in British Columbia. It was a meditative atmosphere that provided time, space, beauty, and quietness. She led us in many exercises that promoted times of reflection and exploring the inner life. The announced day of silence was one of the exercises. My response was, *"They will never believe this at home."* I looked at Nancy, who was the most animated conversationalist in our group. Her eyes were wide and filled with terror. Laughing, I made a mental note to avoid sitting with her during our meals of silence. The next twenty-four hours were quite remarkable, as I noted in the following journal entries:

Tuesday evening—outside in the field. *We started our time of* *silence tonight after Luci concluded our lecture. Gathering our belongings, we departed to our separate cabins without words. Only the sounds of the ending day filled our ears. Birds exchanging quiet evening songs and the crunching of gravel beneath our feet. I noticed that some of us walked with heads down, eyes averted. Others were grinning sheepishly. What is my response? Me? One who has had conversations with cows and clouds and people to whom I have never been introduced? Though some might find it strange, I am anticipating this time of absence in conversation and have actually looked forward to it.*

I've noticed that I have gotten really sensitive to noise after being here on the island. Even tonight, I was sitting by a woman taking notes on her laptop. I found the clicking of keys distracting—the hum of the motor drowning out the happy and contented swishing of my pen as I took notes. Laptops should be banned from classes of an artistic and sensitive nature and exclusively used in technical ones such as systematic theology or accounting. And that is strictly my arrogant opinion submitted with a humble and sincere heart. There is something about an intimate setting such as this that warrants old-fashioned note taking. Tonight I felt remiss in not telling my cabin mates, Amy and Patricia, goodnight. So I wrote them a note and put it on the bathroom mirror.

Goodnight my fellow lambkins, May the Good Shepherd watch over us this night and fill us with His Quiet Sweetness.

Wednesday morning—by the lily pond. *It is as if the world around me is in order this morning. The sun is shining, yet it is cool with intermittent breezes. Just right for a long sleeve t-shirt. We continue our day of silence, only the birds don't know it. They are singing their little hearts out this morning. I saw one carrying away a big red cherry and wanted a picture. No camera. Click the shutter of my heart, Father!*

I want to exclaim to Fran who is opening her window, "Come out!

It's gorgeous!" Instead, I wave exuberantly and blow her a kiss. Karen motions for me to come over for coffee. I want to say, "Thank you! Thank you! Thank You!" Instead we smile together and I squeeze her hand. This morning I find it difficult to be quiet. It's like a big "Hallelujah bubble" wants to float out of my throat!

Our first meal together in our day of silence was most interesting. I saw someone doing sign language, which I thought was cheating! There was an element of slight awkwardness that I sensed among some, including myself. What do you do with your eyes? Stare at your plate? Or out the window? Read? I almost think that reading may take away from the richness of eating in silence—it seems that you should give your mind a break as well. It is interesting listening to the mechanics of eating—swallowing and chewing, a few slurps, the tinging of silverware against the bottom of the bowl. I found myself enjoying these new sounds. When my animated friend and conversationalist, Nancy, didn't show up for lunch, I was concerned. I wrote a note to someone, which I suppose was no different than the person doing sign language: "Do you think Nancy died from not talking?!"

When our time of silence was over, I felt a bit hesitant to let go of what had taken place in my heart and journal. I sensed new stirring and fresh growth in all of us. But this new growth was most evident to me when we had a night of group-sharing from our journals. With tears in my eyes, I listened as Nancy recited hers from memory. Her voice was quiet and steady as she spoke from a deep place within.

Anything is Possible
by Nancy Hoffman

Would you say to a paralyzed man, "Race you to the corner!" or ask a blind man to drive you to the airport?

Would you ask a hearing impaired person to listen to a song
you just wrote
or ask a mute to sing it?
Not unless they are touched by Jesus on earth
or redeemed by God in heaven—
    "Then will the eyes of the blind be opened
    and the ears of the deaf unstopped.
    Then will the lame leap like a deer,
    and the mute tongue shout for joy."
Would you offer water to your wedding guests
when they ask for wine?
Only when Jesus says, "Fill the jars with water."
Would you expect to speak to a man dead four days?
Only when Jesus says, "Come forth."
Would you ask a camel to walk through the eye of a needle?
"With God all things are possible."
Would you ask someone with ADHD
to not speak for 24 hours?
Anything is possible with God, so Help Me God!
Help me concentrate not so much on not talking,
but on listening to You.

As she finished, we sat there in hushed quietness until I
jumped to my feet, applauding her words, her life, and her
God, who had just spoken so profoundly through her.

Silence and quietness provide the opportunity for us to
hear His voice and to sometimes re-acquaint ourselves with
Him, as written in Isaiah 26:20: "Enter your chambers, and
shut your doors behind you; hide yourself, as it were, for a little moment." Times of silence with one another can open up
conversations through the eyes—the windows of one's soul.
Words can be carefully sorted and sifted through as treasures.

We keep some and toss others. But glance into the soul of someone through their eyes and even their silence may speak louder than their words. Look, see beyond the shield and barrier that words sometimes become.

There are voices that we hear in solitude,
but they grow faint and inaudible
as we enter the world.

—*Ralph Waldo Emerson*

Times of silence must sometimes be cultivated and carved into our lives. We sometimes would rather talk and plan and analyze. And there are occasions for those verbal activities. But there are moments when another Voice says, "Be still, and know that I am God" (Psalm 46:10*a*). "In quietness and confidence shall be your strength" (Isa. 30:15*b*). We can't always go to an island to get away from activities and people. But we can go to Him with an attitude of quietness, first of all, and we can create a physical space reserved for Him. In the solitude of His presence, we will become accustomed to His voice. And like Nancy, we will find that all things are possible.

Thanks to Nancy Hoffman for letting me share her poem.

Holy Hugs and Kisses

"I will praise You,
for I am fearfully and wonderfully made."
Psalm 139:14a

Miss Helen Wright is one of the most delightful creatures on this earth. Having just celebrated her 93rd birthday, she continues to embrace the joy of living. This dear woman has adopted countless spiritual children into her life over the last sixty years. In our relationship, I have never found her to sugarcoat issues that some would find "less spiritual" in nature. She once told me that when she was about seventy-five, she had been longing to be hugged and kissed. I was relieved to hear that you still want to kiss when you are in your seventies. My thirtieth birthday had just passed without any marital prospects, and I was encouraged and grateful to know that there was reason for hope.

The story goes that, one day, while alone in her apartment, she prayed out loud, "God, I sure would like to be hugged and kissed today." Now, it was not that she was praying for an illicit affair or anything of that sort; she was simply acknowledging how she felt. And then she went on with her daily business. A few short hours later, the doorbell rang. You are thinking it was some drop-dead gorgeous old geezer who was there to answer Miss Helen's prayer. Shame on you. Actually, I thought the same thing. The delivery man for the local florist was standing there with balloons that read…"Hugs and Kisses!" She clapped her hands in glee when recounting her story.

I was to remember Miss Helen's "Hugs and Kisses" story several years later. I was in the middle of a formidable writing deadline, due the next morning. My editor had firmly suggested some changes to make on a draft. To my dismay, it was going much slower than I had anticipated. Although exhausted, I could not afford to stop writing. My diet for the last several days had consisted of protein bars, coffee, Diet Dr. Pepper, and more coffee. Leaning back in my chair, I reached up to squeeze my shoulders tightly. Every muscle and neuron in my body was screaming of neglect and abuse. The steady ticking of my mantel clock and its hourly chimes were a reminder that midnight was approaching.

Because of the time constraints facing me, I had isolated myself from contact of friends and family until the project was completed. It was the only means of reaching the deadline. But on this final night, I was feeling alienated—entirely alone in the world. I had a tangible longing to be hugged and touched. Not even in a romantic way...just someone to hold me, hug me, and tell me that all would be well. To lie if necessary! If you could have filed my emotional state, it would have been titled: "Overwhelmed and Distraught."

Indeed, indeed, I was at a severe emotional deficit. The continuous rhythmic chant in my mind was unyielding in its cadence: "I just need someone to hug me, to hug me, to hug me."

If you are sick with the flu, you can legitimately call a friend and ask them to bring you chicken soup. But what about just wanting a hug? It's not quite as easy, even with your best girl friends. I didn't need to talk. I needed physical touch. Skin to skin comfort. Most likely my two single male neighbors would have obliged, but they were not at home. After letting out my third shriek of terror and frustration, I decided if I couldn't have a hug, a Diet Dr. Pepper would have to suffice. My supply needed to be replenished.

It was around 9:00 PM when I left for the grocery store. Turning the corner in my neighborhood, I spotted my friend, Gina, sitting on her steps. Screeching to a sudden halt, I jumped out, leaving my car running. Exchanging a quick hello, I said, "Will you please hug me? Just hug me."

Gina is petite and I am not. She looked up at me quietly and thoughtfully moved to the next step to be taller. And then she wrapped her slender arms around me, holding me tightly and warmly for several minutes. I didn't need to explain anything to her. That was convenient because I did not have the energy to explain, nor the vocabulary. I didn't even understand why I felt as I did. As she embraced me, there was a new resurgence of life that began to fill me in a most amazing way. It was not anything she said, because she didn't use words. It was her loving and human touch that I needed—desperately needed.

I've heard that we need eight hugs a day for emotional well being. No wonder I was in a funk. We are fearfully and wonderfully made. Part of that wonder is our need for human touch. The Lord intricately designed us to need one another and to experience the life-giving presence of people who care, not only through words, but through touch.

Ecclesiastes says there is a time to embrace. The laying on of hands in prayers, benedictions, blessings, and consecrations is interwoven throughout the Scriptures. The gift of touch has the power to affirm, encourage, and comfort. Therefore, the deprivation of relationships and human touch can create loneliness and emotional voids. We shouldn't be embarrassed to acknowledge this need that God has placed within each of us.

We do not understand all the mysteries of our faith and Creator. One mystery is the intricate way in which He created us. In pausing a moment to reflect upon our need for one another, take the opportunity to touch and embrace those within your circle of love and affection. Be open to broaden your border by remembering those who are alone, not only at holidays, but all of the many other days that surround them. Those can be just as lonely.

And in the event that you are in need of a physical embrace, by all means, feel free to ask for one. Or invite yourself to dinner with a family of little children who would be delighted to hug and give you lots of drippy kisses. Visit those who have lost spouses or are not able to get out of their homes. If we will reach out to those in need, God will pour so much back into our lives. There is wholesomeness and purity in the need for one another.

As Jesus walked among people...
He reached out.
He touched.
He loved.
He wept.
And He embraced.

His embrace will saturate our hearts as no physical touch can. We need Jesus first and most of all. He understands our longings more than we do. We are the physical extension of Him to those in need. And He uses others as an extension of His arms to enfold us.

There is a time to embrace.

Lightning Bugs

"For You are great, and do wondrous things."
Psalm 86:10a

Leanne and I stood outside her front porch talking about the deep issues of life—those topics that we can expound upon so elaborately as spiritually mature adults. Torrie, her six-year-old daughter, came running toward us from the front yard exclaiming excitedly, "A lightning bug! I found a lightning bug!"

Her nine-year-old brother, who had just come out the front door, yawned and said with all the seasoned apathy of an over-ripe adult, "Aw, what's the big deal. I've seen a *million.*"

Leaning down toward Torrie's glowing face surrounded by her marvelous golden curls, I said, "Torrie, don't ever get too grown up to notice the lightning bugs."

No one points us to the Creator of lightning bugs better than Jesus when He said, "I tell you the truth, unless you change and become like little children, you will never enter the kingdom of heaven" (Matt. 18:3 NIV).

In *The Mystery of Children,* Mike Mason shares his experiences of what his daughter has taught him about childlike faith. "Children hallow small things. A child is a priest of the ordinary, fulfilling a sacred office that absolutely no one else can fill. The simplest gesture, the ephemeral moment, the commonest object all become precious beyond words when touched, noticed, lived by one's own dear child."

There is sweet mystery in childlikeness that can reveal and enhance the many parallels in our faith. If you have matured to such a degree that you can't see them, perhaps you have only grown numerically and need to downsize. Why is it that the creativity of a young mind surpasses that of an adult? Because we have become so sophisticated in our thinking, we often miss the wonder of the world around us. A wise adult can learn to think as a child and see life through their wonder-filled eyes. Time spent in conversation with and in the company of a child whose imagination has not yet been dulled by thankless activities is a creative event in and of itself.

I've heard the average four-year-old laughs four hundred times a day. Knowing the incessant giggles of my own nieces and nephew, I have no trouble believing this statistic. Children aren't concerned with our social statistics and they aren't weighted down with responsibility, nor should they be. But if we shared even a little in their ability to laugh spontaneously, we would be happier and healthier. Surely the Lord thinks laughter is important because He created our bodies to respond to it by releasing chemicals called endorphins, which promote good health.

C. S. Lewis said the Lord wants us to have a child's heart, but a grown-up's head. We can have the maturity that an adult should have as well as childlike joy. Children never postpone the feeling of joy or wait for a more appropriate time to express happiness. They live in the present. Even after a good spanking, they seem to bounce right back into action.

If you have the good fortune to spend time with children, you will notice they have a way of adding the oil of life to our rusty minds. Once I left some of my rust behind in the ditch of a Carolina mountain. My niece Caroline and I spent the afternoon careening down a mountain in North Carolina at breakneck speed in her little red wagon. When the speed got out of control, we plowed into the autumn leaves in a ditch below and lay there giggling. Take every opportunity to rust proof your life with children.

Children are loyal and quick to forgive. They smile and laugh easily and are spontaneous in their affection and trust. They delight in things that we often overlook like roly-poly bugs, lizards, and ice-cream cones. You can hear the quick little intake of breath and see their eyes widen with amazement as they examine new and colorful crayons or watch leaves float down the creek. Their laughter is contagious. Make opportunities to spend time with them; you will see the world a little more clearly through their eyes. Be assured that sometimes they see much more clearly than we do.

Ask the Lord to restore the wonder in your life that you had as a child. "The heavens declare the glory of God," wrote the psalmist (Psalm 19:1a). Sadly enough, much of the world looks at His art with seared eyes, wounded by the garish lights of tinseled and shallow entertainment. His beauty becomes shaded and obscure in the glare of high-tech modernization.

Take a moment to assess the things that you place your attention and eyes upon.

Are they hollow and shallow in the light of His glory? Is your heart more sophisticated than humble and childlike? Does the Creator of butterflies and lightning bugs provoke gratefulness in your heart for His gentle and sweet beauty? He longs to open your eyes to His creation, restoring spontaneous joy and laughter which will erupt from your heart and flow from your lips. The joy of the Lord will draw lives to the saving grace of our Father, not our sophistication.

So if it takes the theology of a lightning bug to illumine the darkness of your stagnated mind, rejoice! Praise Him! And if you still can't find that indescribable joy, ask a child to help you look.

Purity vs. Nose Hair

"Search me, O God, and know my heart...
see if there is any wicked way in me,
and lead me in the way everlasting."
Psalm 139: 23–24

Dinner was over, the floor swept and mopped, and the walls washed down. Perhaps not quite so bad as that, but after spending three weeks with my friends and their four little boys, I was beginning to appreciate motherhood in a new depth. The summons to dinner might as well be the call of the wild. These were great little guys, just not quite coordinated with eating and drinking utensils. But then neither am I.

After dinner it was time for quietness and family devotions. We gathered in the living room. As Jay read from the Bible, I watched the faces of Marnie and her four sons. They listened intently and silently. I marveled at the privilege that had been entrusted to my friends as they were prayerfully raising these little guys to love and serve the Lord. They are missionaries, and I was visiting to help out for a few weeks while they were in language school. Poor Jay was exhausted and happened to have a terrible head cold. It was clearly an effort for him to keep reading.

The rapt attention of four-year-old Greer was especially touching. Nestled under his Daddy's arm, his face intently studied his father's face. His dark brown eyes were somber and reflective. Quietly he sucked his two favorite fingers while holding his blanket in his other arm. My maternal hormones were zipping and zinging everywhere as I absorbed every precious moment of this endearing scenario. I allowed my mind to imagine how each of these boys would grow spiritually and in what ways the Lord would use them. There was a strong sense of significant eternal destiny for each of them.

My eyes wandered back to Greer as he continued to be engrossed in the truth of his father's words. Reaching up to brush welling tears from my eyes, I watched Greer take his fingers from his mouth long enough to blurt, "Mommy, why does Daddy have hair in his nose?" In the brief and pregnant silence, Jay looked at his son in stunned speechlessness. Marnie and I were gasping for breath as we convulsed in laughter. Greer just looked at us in puzzlement.

What Greer did not appreciate was the fact that he was such an articulate reminder of who I am at times. There have been those days when I have bent my head in prayer while my mind was on the sale at my favorite store. Or I have taken notes during a sermon when actually I was making a "to do" list, my harassed mind racing to the events of tomorrow rather than absorbing the truth of the message of the moment. To anyone looking at me, however, I appeared to be the exemplary spiritual parishioner.

Thus we have another revealing moment in the life of the charlatan. That would be me. Guilty. This I cannot deny. Nor can I deny the grace that covers me when my heart is impure. Or those times when I have performed and accomplished formidable tasks for the applause and affirmation of man. Oh how I wish I could redeem those times, for I don't remember the applause—only the exhaustion.

Man's acclaims fade away in the distance in a few brief moments. Proverbs talks about the pleasure of sin as "fleeting." It is momentary, just as the applause of man flees so very quickly. But the blessings of obedience and the affirmation of God, when we have served Him quietly, lasts forever. And on the occasions when our activities or accomplishments are applauded and acclaimed by those whose lives have been touched by ours, I am reminded of Corrie Ten Boom's response to compliments. She said that at the end of a day, she would take the many lovely and kind words that had been showered upon her. As if gathering them together as flowers in her hands, she would hold them before the Lord, offering them to Him for His pleasure as if they were a bouquet of flowers.

Surely that heart attitude of gratefulness must bring joy to the heart of our Father. I must be aware that anything good in my life is because of His grace and is to be received as a gift from Him. Whatever our activities entail, we must remind ourselves, if necessary, that man looks at the outward appearance but God looks at our hearts. Do we want to please man or God? Sometimes my answer is man, which looks as foolish and absurd on paper as it is. Ridiculous.

Little Greer was not being deceptive the night of his inquiry about his Daddy's nose hair. He was being obedient in his quietness until his curiosity blurted out!

Search me, O God. Bring to my attention my pious, self-righteous acts. Reveal to me anything that I do for my own exaltation. For You are the only One to be praised. May my heart be pure before You, and when my true self does blurt out unexpectedly, may I not cover or try to hide it, but allow You to remove it from my life.

The Best Prom Date

"Surely goodness and mercy
shall follow me all the days of my life;
and I will dwell in the house of the Lord forever."
Psalm 23:6

High school memories are something of a blur to me. One event is highlighted, however. My parents told me that I couldn't date until I was sixteen, which was really *quite* optimistic of them. It was nice in theory, but in reality, I wasn't exactly the date queen of Tuscaloosa County High. Not that it had anything to do with my looks...though of this I am not entirely sure. My greatest torment at that time was my naturally curly hair. Straight was in, which was a disadvantage for me. My mother was sadly deceived into believing that men liked women with long hair, so she insisted that I keep my hair long. After sleeping on orange juice cans all night, my hair would be somewhat straight until I walked out into the humidified air of Alabama. After that it was a challenge to stand next to me in the hall. This is also the time that my feet took on an accelerated rate of growth. I was known to stumble frequently while walking down the hall, not making me the most outstanding dance partner. This feature is one a young man would take into consideration in asking a date to the Spring Prom.

The only person I wanted to go with was Buster Abernathy. What a debonair name for an eighteen-year-old. I am sure he grew into it. He was sweet and cute in a bear cub sort of way. But he invited Marcia Perry, who was adorable, petite, and darling. And who had cuter hair than I did. Much cuter. Besides, I don't think he even knew I existed except as someone in his

English Lit class. I just admired him from afar with a wistful heart. There was the time that I almost fell in his lap when I tripped going to my desk, but I don't think he recognized me because of the color of my face. Those were the days that I used to blush every time I stumbled. Now I just get up and keep on going.

On the day of the prom, it was the tradition for all the girls to go home after lunch to have their hair coiffed and nails done. Sitting around in our sparse debate class that afternoon, I decided that if Buster Abernathy was so shallow as to invite someone who was petite and had cute hair, it was a good thing I found out before we got serious or anything like that. And why should I miss a great evening because of his superficiality?

The prom started at 7:00. After getting out of school at 3:00, I stopped at the local florist and ordered myself a corsage. After arriving home, I announced to my mother that I was going to the prom after all. She was excited until I told her I was going with myself and asked if I could use the car that night. Fortunately I had a dress for the occasion. Ironing my hair and setting it with enough hair spray to make it flammable, I donned my dress and departed, leaving a cloud of perfume behind me.

Driving into my high school parking lot and seeing all the guys in tuxedos with their dates in tow, I began to feel daunting apprehensions. Wishing I had at least taken our brown station wagon to the car wash, I patted my corsage for reassurance. Walking amidst all the couples, I smiled as if it were entirely normal to be at a prom alone. I even argued with the guy at the door that my ticket should be half price since I was not a couple. I mean, it was bad enough to have to buy my own ticket, but to have to pay for some imaginary man who was too shallow and obtuse to invite me? Really, a girl has to draw her boundaries somewhere.

My misgivings faded as the evening turned into one that Ginger Rogers might have dreamed of. It was a *wonderful* night! I drove my happy self home without any mishap. Hanging my corsage on my bulletin board like all the other girls did who had dates, I was perfectly content to place mine among the other teenage memoirs.

Opportunity dances with those already on the dance floor.

—H. Jackson Brown, Jr.

Psalm 23 has a nugget of truth that is especially worth pulling from all the others for a moment. "Thou art with me." God will put a companion in our lives sometimes, whether for marriage, travel, or even a prom date. Sometimes He does not. He is our companion. I've had many travel and ministry opportunities that I would not have participated in if I had waited on someone to go with me. I went alone, except...He was with me! And He sent *goodness* and *mercy* to follow me! Together we embarked upon the great adventures He had in store.

Although a prom night without a date may seem a bit trivial, looking back, I believe God was building in me a quality called, to use a Yiddish word, *chutzpah*: boldness, confidence, the willingness to try something new and different. And that has been the foundation for so many opportunities, not only those that presented themselves to me, but ones that I have pursued. Yes, it can be very nice to have someone to travel with. However, if there is no one, He will not only unsparingly give you the grace to venture out of the status quo way of doing something, He will also be with you. And He will send goodness and mercy as your travel companions, your rear guard!

We can live a life that is unrestrained in exploring His will—being willing to venture out beyond the average, to go beyond that which makes us comfortable. The other option is to live a life that is always predictable. Webster's Dictionary defines *predictable* as, "ordinary, mundane, common, unremarkable, unexceptional, routine."

In other words…Dull!

Exchange ordinary living for *extra*ordinary! Take some new risks in exploring life and God-given opportunities. You will not be alone. Tagging along right beside you are your two best traveling companions, Goodness and Mercy!

Dearly Beloved

"To my dear friend Gaius,
whom I love in truth."
3 John 1, NIV

O nce while sitting in the Asheville, North Carolina airport, I felt overwhelmed by the task I was working on. Opening my journal, I penned a description of my harried state: *Here I am with all my bags. I am weighed down with all my stuff, assorted Christmas cards, three address books, and a Rolodex of assorted addresses. Good grief.*

This particular task happened to be my Christmas correspondence. The date was December 28th. I was returning home from our Christmas family get-together and was just starting to work on my holiday cards.

Unfortunately, my frustration with communication does not always center around the holidays. It is a twelve-month struggle and has always been unusually problematic for me. I have an unrealistic habit of trying to keep in contact with a ridiculously high number of people whom I may have met on a missions trip, an airplane, or in a grocery store. The simple act of writing a note of thanks or encouragement becomes a monumental task when I consider having to locate the slip of paper on which I've jotted down the needed address. It's difficult to keep up with who is who, who is with whom, and how many *whos* they now have.

If I would learn to write short and simple notes, I am quite sure my correspondence would not be so overwhelming. But more often I write the way I talk, thus saying way too much and taking too long.

Oh, the lost opportunities of letter writing—the ones I have composed in my heart but never on paper. The ones I wrote on paper but never mailed.

Letter writing is the only device
for combining solitude with good company.

—*Lord Byron*

In this last year I have sincerely petitioned for divine help in this area. And He has been helping me nibble away at this mountain by making just one small commitment: to try to write just one note a day. Not even a letter, but a note. Until I catch up, I sometimes try to double or triple the number of notes I write, and I am taking heart as I see progress. Correspondence is becoming more of a habit. To do this at least four days a week is an obtainable goal, one that I am actually enjoying.

And this year, for Christmas, I have found the perfect card. It is simple and decorated only with an isolated snowflake. The inscription reads: *Late holiday greetings from your favorite flake.*

With a relieved conscience, I can enjoy my holiday correspondence after the New Year! In this electronic age of email, we might not be so hasty to pen a letter. But there is nothing that takes the place of a handwritten letter that someone you care about can keep tucked away in a sachet box of special memoirs. It takes a few moments of your time, this is true. But knowing the joy and warmth that someone will receive from your written words of love and affirmation will perhaps encourage you to take up pen and paper. Just as the apostle John did: "To my dear friend, Gaius."

Beyond Ourselves

"Ask of me, and I shall give thee the heathen
for thine inheritance."
Psalm 2:8a, KJV

My companion and I walked into the foyer of the ornate
and lovely sanctuary. It was Sunday morning and the
grandson of one of my patients was with me. It was the first
time in my life that I had ever been embarrassed to be in
church. Making my way toward the back rather than my usual
seat up front, I prayed I would not see anyone I knew. People
sent curious glances toward me and my companion. Even now,
I vividly recall the sense of being different and out of place—
unequal.

This young man and I had shared some deep conversations
about life and death. His heart was searching for truth and I
invited him to our church worship service. He told me that he
didn't have anything to wear. "Oh, it doesn't matter what you
wear," I enthusiastically told him. He didn't look convinced.

"Listen," I said, "if it will make you more comfortable, I will
wear jeans and a t-shirt."

He agreed, but seemed rather dubious.

I am sorry to say that it did matter. Not to Jesus, I am quite
sure. But the other parishioners appeared to be uncomfortable and troubled to have someone so different in their midst.
The ushers were awkward in their manner of greeting us. And
I was embarrassed for my friend and for the church. But most
of all, I was disappointed in myself as my own shallowness and
pride were undeniably revealed to me.

The events of our national tragedy on September 11, 2001 prompted me to recall that Sunday morning service from more than ten years ago. Only a few days before the terrorist attack, I had been reflecting upon the meaning of revival. Many wonderful songs have been written asking the Lord to "bring us revival." My question to the Lord had been, "What are we singing about, Lord? What are we asking You to do?" Some would think revival is a particular week of church marked on the calendar: "Scheduled Meetings—Revival."

Is it not true for the last several years that our churches have been praying for spiritual renewal? For revival to take place in our nation? My question to you is, Are you prepared for this to happen? Do you know what you are asking God to do? I'm asking myself the very same question.

I spoke with pastors of several denominations. They say that revival is described, based upon Scripture and church history, as a movement of the Holy Spirit in which there is repentance and renewal of spiritual hunger. There is a turning away from the allure of the world while asking God to purify our hearts, motives, and desires. This is not only true for a new Christian but for us older ones as well. For who could deny that many faithful attendees of church have become stagnant in religious doctrine, possibly committed more to an order of worship or calendar of events than they are to Him?

Since September 11, we have seen the Lord's hand do wonderful things, indeed. Our nation has loosened its grip on so many things that have stifled our hunger for Him. People have begun to examine their hearts and to assess their lives. Churches were filled to capacity the Sunday after the darkest day in the history of our nation. It was reported that attendance was record-breaking in numbers.

As wonderful as it is to see the Lord stirring and provoking hearts, again I ask, are we ready to receive those whom He will bring into the doors of our hallowed churches? It's like standing on the beach and watching what the tide brings in. We are not prepared for what might come washing in unexpectedly. What if someone comes into your church who has multiple tattoos and looks different than you do? What if their body is pierced in many interesting places? Are you ready to love them and show warmth and acceptance? What if they are involved in homosexuality and desire cleansing and deliverance? Are you ready to be a signpost pointing them to the Deliverer? What if they are a challenge to your olfactory senses? Yes, they *stink*. Will you sit by them or put them in a designated corner? Perhaps they will be dressed in something not exactly in the confines of conservatism. Will you judge or embrace? Can you offer compassion for those who have had abortions and need not only forgiveness but healing? What if they are a different nationality? A different color?

I can only imagine the voices of those who might be filled more with religion than love exclaiming, "Oh my…it just can't be!"

If you are not ready to receive the least of these as Jesus would, you might need to take some time of preparation, for I assure you, the tide is coming in! Thanks be to God for ripping off our religious facades and letting us see who we really are. I saw who I was that day as I cowered in the back pew, ashamed to be seen with someone different. We take a risk of being criticized and ill-received when we associate with the "least of these." Would you rather have the approval of someone who would judge or the approval of your heavenly Father?

The church has often been compared to a hospital where we are to receive the sick and wounded. That sounds really sweet, and I believe that there is tremendous truth in that comparison. But as someone who has worked in the medical profession, let me assure you, there is an incredible amount of challenging things that happen before a patient is discharged as a whole person. There are full bedpans, offensive odors, infections, wounds, and unappealing tasks. A patient needs assistance to become independent, and we must sometimes take care of basic needs while they are being healed.

The parallels are fairly obvious, I trust. To love with the compassion and faithfulness of a holy God can only be done in His strength and with His heart. We can't fake it or pretend. If your heart is repulsed by the things I have just described, follow the words of the prophet Hosea: "Sow for yourselves righteousness; reap in mercy; break up your fallow ground, for it is time to seek the Lord, till He comes and rains righteousness on you" (Hosea 10:12).

Sometimes I want to flinch, although this is not a proud admission. Recently, I had the opportunity to give someone a ride to a bus station. Afterwards, I left my windows down all day to rid my car of the odor. Yet God graced me with joy in providing help for this person, and even allowed me to find extra money I had stashed away to share with her. It brought joy to me and I had a wonderful opportunity to pray with and encourage one who had experienced very unfortunate circumstances. Who is to say that I wouldn't be in the same place if my paths had not been ordered as they are? And the same applies to you. We just sometimes forget. This is a reminder to me as well.

He has extended grace into our lives so that we can pour freely into others. These upcoming days will provide the opportunity for you to be stretched and pulled out of your comfort zones. Hallelujah! Thanks be to God, who wants us to be as fresh and supple as new wineskins. Don't just get your toes wet...be immersed in His Spirit!

Ask Him for the agnostic, the heretic, the pagan, the homo-sexual, the Muslim, and the religious sinner, commonly known in the Bible as "the heathen." Invest in an inheritance that is bigger than the stock market or IRAs. Eternal rewards. He desires to gives us the heathen as our inheritance. The down and out *and* the up and out. The perfumed and prissy ones *and* the ones who are repugnant to our noses and pride.

Ask of Him.

A Day in the Cemetery

"So teach us to number our days,
that we may gain a heart of wisdom."
Psalm 90:12

Wiping the tears from my eyes, I blew my nose and answered the phone with a tremulous, "Hello?" It was my sister, Sunnie. Alarmed to hear my tearful voice, she quickly asked what was wrong. Upon hearing the explanation for my tears, she burst into laughter. My eardrums recoiled from the resonating shrieks of her mirth. Now I certainly enjoy a good titter with anyone, but today I was a bit miffed at her. In response to her question, I had replied that I was planning my funeral. In the process, I found it so touching and beautiful that I had burst into tears. Alright…I can readily admit that my tears were a bit overboard, but they were, nevertheless, genuine. I was not crying at the thought of dying, but because I wouldn't be there to enjoy it with all my friends! It *really* was such a lovely service.

This funeral program was not written in relation to any sickness I was having, nor was it prompted by depression. Actually, I was in quite a good mood when I started it. Let me ask you to pause for a moment. Would you allow someone other than yourself to take charge in the planning of important events of your life such as a wedding or any other major celebration? For most of us the answer is a resounding "no." So why would you want an event that is only second in importance to being born to be planned without your input? Who wants to die and just show up in a box or an urn? Absurd! Ridiculous!

Times of reflection about my mortal end started a number

of years ago. On one of those younger twenty-something birth-days, I drove to the quiet countryside where my favorite grand-father is buried. Since I was a child when he died, my memo-ries of him are few but sweet. As I walked around the old ceme-tery in my fresh and philosophical mindset, I pondered life and death as I wrote in my journal. My conclusion from that reflective outing was, "We live in order that we may die. Each second of our lives is closer to that which is eternal. That is why we were given life in the first place."

If you have never spent any time in a cemetery, perhaps a leisurely stroll on a nice day would be an outing worthy of your time. There are not just names engraved on a stone—they rep-resent a life filled with all the same emotions and dreams that we have.

Sometimes, even without the provocation of a cemetery stroll, in the middle of all my flurry, I have felt that longing to think about life…life *before* death and life *after* death. And just for the record again, these occasions were not provoked by depression, unexpected weight gain, or the breakup of a relationship.

I have a vast repertoire of foolish time wasters, but I believe the moments that I have thought about leaving this world are not wasted. My favorite visit to a cemetery in New York was thankfully recorded in my journal. I was grateful to come upon these thoughts, for they reminded me of a rich and meaning-ful afternoon. My journal entry that day sounds like I was speaking to someone. Upon reading it later, I realized the Holy Spirit was speaking to *me*. I hope that it will speak to you.

*"I am on a picnic today. My lunch includes a pint of milk complete with **sixteen** grams of milk fat, hand-squeezed from a dairy farm in Poughkeepsie, New York, an egg sandwich with dill pickles, and a*

lovely view of an old cemetery. Mark Twain and his beloved Olivia and their children are resting only a few feet away on this brilliant fall day in Elmira, New York. Two fathers and their children are walking nearby hand in hand. One little one with ringlets is kicking the autumn leaves while giggling. A moment to relish and enjoy as I sit here surrounded by the remains of the dead and loving it. I can't help but think about the reality of death.

Living to Die.

We are born to prepare to die in recognizing that our years, our days, and our hours are a gift and from no one other than God alone. Our times, our words, our conversations, our business activities, and all that we do are a gift. Oh, that we would be ever so mindful of our need of Him. Ever so grateful for the gift He has given, the gift of life now and for eternity. Our days are as fleeting moments. Max Lucado said it is a good idea before making a major decision to take a walk in a cemetery. How does the weight of that decision affect what really matters? But even just as important, what of our daily life decisions, those that pertain to our relationships with others, character issues, and words that should be spoken or not spoken? Life does not wait on us and Death does not delay. Is it more important to write a letter the old fashioned way or catch a sale at the mall? To spend time in quietness reading a good book or even writing a good book? An ice cream cone with a child or baking cookies for someone that is lonely? Or what about updating your prayer journal? Let us evaluate the activities of our lives and not be as ants that run constantly. Quietness, peace, and solitude. So when it is time for us to lay at rest as all of my surrounding companions, we will die with peace in our hearts and not exhausted. I don't want to die tired and frantic, but able to enjoy even that moment. I don't want the regret of unfinished letters or unfinished books. All the cute clothes and "perfect outfits" will eventually be tossed, but kind deeds along the way will be as seeds that I love to plant in my gardens. They do grow and produce and multiply into the lives of others. And so may it be with our lives that we live with the daily hope of reproducing the life of Christ to others. To share a kind deed, a smile, a gentle touch, a warm embrace. Hold your "To Do" lists before the Father, and ask Him to let them be like the wheat and the chaff and to keep only that which is good.

A magnificent oak tree is in front of me. It casts its shadow on many who lay in rest at its roots. How many lives it has seen make their final earthly journey? The tears that this beautiful earth has received as loved ones left behind have wept. Only that which is eternal is lasting. Teach us to number our days. So that we might present to Thee a heart of wisdom, so that when we do make our final journey, we can say it is well with our soul and not, oh, I need to pick up just one more thing at the mall. Right now I am not going to the mall. As autumn leaves are wafting gently from above, I am going to close my eyes and take a little nap. It is respectfully quiet here."

When my father died, I emailed friends who were walking the long and dark road with us as we watched him leaving. "Dad is not doing well. They have encouraged us to call the family and said we have a few days." Actually, all of our days are numbered, it's just that we are more aware of the reality at this time. "He that dwelleth in the secret place shall abide under the shadow of the Almighty. Please pray that we stay in the Shadow. In His eternal embrace, Angela."

As painful as death is, I believe the greater grief is not preparing for it. Can this be a gentle reminder for you to reflect upon why we are here and where we are going?

Henri Nouwen once said, "Dying is a continual process—not a sudden interruption, but a dynamic dimension of living in each moment. We should not be surprised when suffering and death come. Life is a school in which we are trained to depart."

Our lives in this world as we know it and all of our many wonderful adventures can be compared to what C. S. Lewis said in his epic Chronicles of Narnia: "This is only the cover and title page. One day we will begin Chapter One of the Great Story. And that will be the story that is more wonder-filled than our hearts could ever contain." We can daily experience His joy and fullness of life, even in the midst of pain, knowing that we can all look forward to truly living happily ever after. There will not be an ending to our story but, rather, the Beginning—Forever and Ever.

The Praying Fish

"As for me, I will call upon God,
and the Lord shall save me.
Evening and morning and at noon I will pray,
and cry aloud, and He shall hear my voice."
Psalm 55:16–17

I looked at my watch as I knelt in the chapel. Thirty minutes with the Lord. It was about three o'clock in the morning. Although it sounds saintly that I was up at that time to pray, it had nothing to do with my level of spirituality. I was taking my break from a midnight shift of nursing. One of the nicest features of working that difficult shift is that I would often go to the chapel in the hospital and pray. It was usually empty and quiet. Once while working in a Catholic hospital, I chose one of the confessional booths to pray in. Someone came into the quiet chapel and fell asleep while I watched with amusement from my screened alcove.

Now, as I knelt in prayer at three in the morning, I too drifted off to sleep. Waking up abruptly, I looked at my watch and realized I had been "praying" for almost an hour. Jumping up in a frenzy, I was horrified to find myself falling over to the floor in an ungraceful wad. It felt like someone had come in during my prayer/nap time and amputated my legs below the knees. Frantically I tried to jump up again, and once more I fell back helplessly. Still in a daze because of having awakened so abruptly, all I could think was that I felt and looked like a flopping fish.

As much as I love to pray, sometimes I feel that I am about as effective as a flailing and flopping wide-mouth bass. I just don't seem to be getting anywhere. But even the night that I was slumbering instead of praying, I am confident that He heard the prayers of my heart, and probably even smiled upon me as a parent does a sleeping child.

What of those moments when I am awake and would rather *think* about praying than doing it? Those are the times when I can't pay attention to my feelings. Satan will throw in all the interference necessary to stop us from bending our hearts and knees to the Lord. At times we are eager to pray. It is something we look forward to. But sometimes the thought of praying is as inviting as chewing on Kleenex. Or is that just me?

Once I spent some time alone at a friend's log cabin in the woods. I was talking to the Lord about my disappointment in myself in the discipline of prayer. It seemed that I was more interested in sleeping than getting up early enough to have time with Him.

Pulling out my journal, I began to write as He was speaking to me while I sat quietly in front of the fireplace.

Angela, the very things in your life that you might think are self-imposed, discipline and obedience, are actually the very commandments that I have put in your heart. Remind yourself of these things. As a loving parent instructs his child in acts of obedience, so I have called you to a lifestyle of obedience. A lifestyle cannot be incorporated unless you first start on a day to day basis. Hear Me, child. Respond in eagerness. Fill your heart, mind, spirit, and soul with Me. I desire that you might have sensitive ears to hear the things of My Spirit. You have pulled away from the pain of discipline. Embrace all of Me, including discipline. For this is part of Me also. Choose life, not the sleep of death.

Whew. Well, that was a wake-up call. Similar to one of those bugle reveilles at summer camp. Loud and Clear. And it was one for which I was most grateful. So often I crave the soft and pampered life much more than the disciplined one. It is some-times easier to make decisions based on our feelings and emo-tions rather than what the Lord is drawing us to do. At times prayer feels mundane—no excitement. That is why we are often more eager to do something proactive, foolishly forget-ting that *prayer is proactive!* Another journal entry reveals some of my absurd thoughts.

Although it doesn't make a bit of sense to me, it is sometimes easier for me to leap out of bed to catch a plane to a foreign country...to be subjected to a third world environment...than to jump out of bed and pray. Let me heed the words of Oswald Chambers regarding early morning prayer: "Get up now and think about it later."

It is all a process, and many mornings I have thrown my alarm under the bed instead of getting up. But prayer is not limited to just the morning. Evening and morning and after-noon will I pray, writes the psalmist. We have all those moments in between to have an attitude and lifestyle of prayer. Even when you would almost rather chew Kleenex than pray, remind yourself who is attempting to stop you from sharing intimate time with the Lord. Just do it and think about it later!

Lord, You Are Making Me Nervous

"'For with God nothing will be impossible.'
Then Mary said, 'Behold the maidservant of the Lord!
Let it be to me according to your word.'"
Luke 1:37–38

Although I have not experienced pregnancy, there was a time when I feared my water would break. I was at the Christmas pageant at one of the largest churches in my city. One of the directors had observed me doing a monologue of Mary and asked if I would be part of their Christmas Eve performance. At the time, it had seemed like a pleasant opportunity. But now, as I waited to go out on stage to a church that was filled to capacity, it seemed like a very terrible idea, indeed. Four thousand people. Eight thousand eyeballs.

Oh dear, dear, dear.

I regretted that I had ever opened my big mouth in agreement to perform this part. I didn't even have the customary Christmas donkey to hang onto for support. It was one of those *just me and Jesus* moments. Feeling like I needed to empty my bladder for the umpteenth time, the thought occurred that maybe my water really would break after I got on stage. "Oh Loooord," I moaned out loud.

The maintenance man, who was walking by in my moment of travail and groaning, stopped in concern.

"Are you okay?" he asked kindly.

"Noooooo."

I continued my thoughts aloud to my new sympathetic

friend. "You know, we would be fools to think we can do anything without Him. Because if He doesn't abundantly, supernaturally, and extravagantly help me, I am sunk. Seriously sunk. In front of all those people, not only do I have the potential of forgetting my lines and falling on my face *and* my protruding abdomen, but I just know my water is going to break."

He enthusiastically, yet compassionately agreed with me. What logical man would have the courage to disagree with a pregnant woman, even if she is the mother of Jesus?

Jesus did help me. Kindly and graciously, He helped me ever so dearly. After I waddled across the stage and began speaking, my heart and mind were transported to a cold night in Bethlehem. For a few tender moments, I imagined what it must have been like for Mary and as she anticipated the birth of her son and Savior. It was no longer a performance. The words of the young mother of my Savior were bigger to me than the vast audience before me.

Pause for a moment and reflect upon the response of Mary to Gabriel, the divine messenger who had so abruptly interrupted her life. This young girl, whose heart was most likely quaking in fear and whose mind was racing with questions, responded with a trusting heart: "Be it unto me according to your word. Let there be a performance of all that you have spoken."

She didn't argue or question His divine plan for her life. She was willing. Mary followed this declaration by offering her praises and worship to the Lord. Gabriel had ended his announcement to her with words that surely she was clinging to.

"Nothing shall be impossible with God."

The truth of those words covered a young girl's heart like a canopy of grace and peace. They will for us, too, when He *divinely interrupts* our lives. He brings those unexpected opportunities to share the hope within us. We are to speak when our heart is pounding in fear whether it is to one person or five thousand.

The Lord seems to take great delight in reminding me that I can do nothing apart from Him. So often I have had the sensation that He was putting me into situations in which I might know my acute need of Him. It is similar to the sensation that one might have when drowning. He then seems to enjoy the rescue, but not nearly as much as I enjoy being rescued.

Many opportunities have been afforded to me in the area of ministry that have *stretched* me way out of my comfort zone—something similar to what it must feel like to grow into a pair of maternity pants. You just never imagined that you could expand to such enormous proportions.

Perhaps the occasion for ministry will be unplanned. Or possibly, as with my night as Mary, you will have time for preparation. In this particular example, I was asked and was willing. It seemed to be a wonderful opportunity to share in celebration of Christmas. I don't remember the applause, but there is warmth in my heart as I recall His presence that was so near to me that night.

He is to be trusted to graciously help and assist us in whatever task He has called us to perform. And like Mary, we can say, "Be it unto me, according to Thy will." And we add, "my voice, my hands, my body—may they all be used to glorify you, O Father."

For nothing shall be impossible with God.

Here Am I Lord, Send Me—Unless You Can Find Somebody Else

*"For ye shall go out with joy,
and be led forth with peace."*
Isaiah 55:12, KJV

In the wake of the tragic terrorist attack upon the US on September 11, 2001, America declared war on the Taliban regime in Afghanistan. Many Christians had already been praying for the release of two young American women who were being held in an Afghan prison. They had been arrested on the charges of religious proselytizing, certainly a very serious offense in a closed Muslim nation. Prayers intensified as thousands of Christians petitioned the only true God to protect and release Heather Mercer and Dayna Curry. Six weeks later, their radiant faces were seen across millions of television screens as America received back two of its daughters. Their account was dramatic as they related the events of their three-month imprisonment and their close escape. They literally fled for their lives, even burning some of their clothing as a means of being sighted by rescuers.

These two single women had counted the cost of going to a nation closed to the Gospel. Upon their arrest, they knew that the very same God who had led them to Afghanistan would remain with them, giving courage and grace. They went into that Muslim nation with His joy, and their countenances reflected an even greater joy as they spoke of possibly returning one day to the nation that had held them captive. Dayna and Heather said they came to the realization while in prison that if they died, they would die for His glory. If they lived, they would live for His glory.

I openly wept as I closely followed the stories of these two women. My heart was provoked with the desire that I would hold onto my life as loosely as they did. The question was before me: would I be obedient to go wherever He desired to send me? Would I be as yielding and eager to go to a nation that is closed to Christianity as I am to go on a great vacation?

You see, the greatest problem is *me*. I sometimes love my life and its comforts too much. Certainly there is not a shortage of ministry opportunities. It's only a matter of choosing and following His leading, of being obedient in whatever area of ministry He might be provoking within you. I once heard someone say, "God wants to walk around in our bodies." Perhaps He wants to walk through you to other countries or through the doors of a crisis pregnancy center. If you have been going to Bible studies all your life, could this be the time that you lead one?

If your heart is provoked to want to be used unconditionally, ask the Lord to open your heart to the many venues of ministry opportunities. You might be surprised to see the many ways God can use you. For instance, have you ever thought of hospitality as a means of ministry? One of the most impacting conversations I ever had was with a woman in Japan. She was an American, my age, and also single. We were attending a GoFest conference sponsored by Youth With A Mission. My sister and I had just completed a trip into China where we had brought Bibles to the Christians there.

During that time, I was asking the Lord serious questions about my calling into missions. There was a desire to be involved in ministry full time, but I was very unclear of direction. My new friend and I discussed some of the issues I was struggling with. I expressed to her my love for hospitality. One of my greatest joys was in opening my heart and home to people and providing food and fellowship and a relaxed atmosphere for conversation and encouragement. I was afraid that if I went to what we know as the mission field, I would not be able to continue doing what I loved.

She smiled knowingly at me and explained that she knew exactly how I was feeling. Susan was on leave from her work in a refugee camp in Cambodia. Although she was involved in the lives of the orphans, she said one of her greatest contributions to the ministry was through her teapot. She explained that many of the workers would come in from the fields at the end of a long day. She would serve them warmth, comfort, and encouragement from her teapot as she poured hot fragrant tea for them.

Since that conversation, I have embraced what some might look down upon as a "less spiritual" gift. My numerous mission trips always seem to find me in the kitchen chopping up something or serving. Hospitality is just one wonderful channel for our natural creativity and homemaking inclinations. We can easily lose our focus if our intentions become overshadowed by wanting to be the perfect hostess, rather than simply wanting to serve.

The opportunities afforded us are endless. One that has particularly caught the attention of my life is through the sponsorship of children. While once at a nationally known women's conference, a presentation was being made for World Vision, a widely recognized and respected relief organization. I was literally appalled to see a great number of the women leaving during the appeal. They were not exiting quietly, but rather laughing and chatting while on their way to lunch. For the price of a compact disc or a few cups of coffee, we can make the difference in the life of a child. A life or death difference. Literally. Although I don't have natural children of my own, I have two little ones named Dimur and Elsie who live in Guatemala. My mother has twelve additional children, which makes me so grateful for her giving heart. If everyone just adopted one child, what an incredible difference we would make.

If you have been one like me who finds it easier to be first and foremost concerned for "me and mine," ask God to give you a heart for the people and issues that go beyond *you*. I once wrote, *I find it easiest to pray and think about me.* **Me. Me. Me.** *The Kingdom of Angela.* As we ask God to enlarge our hearts—going beyond ourselves—we find the strength of spirit, mind, and emotion to enter boldly before the throne of grace on behalf of nations and people. Ask Him what you might do to make an eternal difference in lives. "Ask, and you will receive, that your joy may be full" (John 16:24*b*).

Perhaps He will lead you to another nation. Most importantly, may each of us come to that place of surrender. Ask to see the world through His eyes. Sometimes the first step is "Lord, I am willing to be willing." He doesn't drag us around to do His will, but He walks beside us, encouraging us along the way. You are not alone on this journey. For the very one who desires that you live as an extension of Him is the One who has called you.

"You shall go out with joy and be led forth with peace." I have a feeling you are going to enjoy the journey!

Acknowledgments

Angela's Concise "Thank You"s

My last Acknowledgments have been compared to an over-enthusiastic female recipient at the Academy Awards who wants to mention every single wonderful person in her life. Although I will not attempt to include such a lengthy list at this time, I do have one, indeed. If you would like to see if your name is on it, please let me know!

So many friends have been faithful to pray and encourage me along the way of this writing process, and for each I am grateful. However, there have been several specific ones who have steadfastly prayed for me in this process of writing. They are Helen Brock, Connie Cortez, Dena Lowery, Karen Berger, Jean Madden, Ginger Combs, Vanessa Vienna, Stephanie Grissom, Melinda McGrath, and Mrs. Beau Miller. You have been like Holy Spirit speed bumps when I was out of control, kindly pointing me to my source of grace. You are each amazing.

And most special thanks to Amy Clifford, who read and suggested and listened and gave. New friend—dear friend—always friend.

To my family—remember all those really nice things I said about you in *Living Every Single Moment*? Ditto! You are still the greatest. You have loved me. You have prayed. You are praying. I am grateful. A wise man would marry me just to get into our family. I must express special thanksgiving for our newest arrival: Miss Emma Kate Henry. Welcome, sweet little girl. We are so glad that you finally came into our hearts and lives. You were long-anticipated but worth the wait!

Betty Watkins is a wonderful mother to her own five children as well as to countless spiritual children. What a privilege for me to be one. Your warm embraces, encouraging life-giving words, and your prayers are interwoven in every page of this book. You not only opened your home to me but your heart as well. And that is a very nice place to be. I love you, Betty.

Lynn DeShazo sings of One who is more precious than silver...and she is too. Thank you, my friend, for your songs that so often accompanied my late night ponderings, reminding me of why I was writing. He used you for much more than getting me out of a speeding ticket!

To all the great folks at New Hope Publishers, my special thanks. Although you sometimes laugh at my suggestions while tossing them, I continue to have very affectionate feelings toward you. Really! I am privileged to know and work with you, and especially my editor, Leslie Caldwell. Again, heartfelt applause to each involved in this project.

And there would not be a book if not for a reading audience. Thanks for reading my stories. If they have encouraged you in any way, I am grateful. Please come and say hi to me at www.angelapayne.com. And thanks most and above all to my Lord Jesus, who daily covers my life with His canopy of love and grace. Amazing God. Amazing Grace. Thank you, Abba Father.

Also by Angela Payne

Living Every Single Moment
1-56309-765-6 • $9.99

***W**hat is a single woman's response to a world teeming with couplehood?* Today's single woman has abundant options for living the full life that Christ came for her to have. Many women consciously or subconsciously shift big plans into neutral until "real" life starts once they are married. In her witty style, Payne guides single women to see the numerous issues they face through the possibilities God has for them.

This book is a passport for any woman who is still waiting for her life to begin. It's a ticket to embrace adventure and love life, laughter, and the Lord.

–NICOLE JOHNSON, actress and author of *Fresh-Brewed Life*

———⟨∞⟩———

Available in Christian bookstores everywhere.

New Hope Publishers

Equipping You to Share the Hope of Christ